the celtic way of life

First published 1976
O'Brien Educational
11 Clare Street, Dublin 2
©

THE CURRICULUM DEVELOPMENT UNIT

The Curriculum Development Unit was established in September 1972. It is sponsored by the City of Dublin Vocational Education Committee and works in co-operation with the School of Education in Trinity College, Dublin, with the approval of the Department of Education. It has a steering committee composed of representatives of these three bodies.

The unit has concentrated on the curricular areas of Humanities, Science and Outdoor Education.

THE HUMANITIES TEAM

Tony Crooks	*(1972)*
Nora Godwin	*(1973)*
Agnes McMahon	*(1975)*
Unit Director:	*Anton Trant*

The collection Celtic Society has been edited for publication by **Agnes McMahon.**

Prior to the publication, the following schools were involved in the development, use and revision of the collection. The suggestions and comments of the teachers in these schools have been used as a basis for the edition:

Colaiste Eanna, Cabra; Colaiste Eoin, Finglas; Coolmine Community School, Clonsilla; Scoil Ide, Finglas; Vocational School, Ballyfermot; Vocational School for Boys, Clogher Road; Vocational School, Crumlin Road.

Illustrations Jeanette Dunne
Cover Design Jarlath Hayes
Printed by E. & T. O'Brien Ltd.
11 Clare Street Dublin 2.

Previous page –
PENDANT, made of
tinned bronze was probably
suspended at the end of a leather strap. Found
on Feltrim Hill near Malahide, Co. Dublin, it
dates to 4th century A.D.

the celtic way of life

THE O'BRIEN PRESS

11 CLARE ST DUBLIN 2

11 CLARE ST DUBLIN 2

contents

the ulster cycle

5

who were the celts?

HE CELTS came from Central Europe, an area east of the river Rhine and north of the Alps, the lands now called Bavaria and Bohemia. They were a farming people, brave and warlike, and from time to time groups of them would set out to find new lands to settle and people to conquer. They spread out in all directions, into France and Spain in the west, into Ireland and Britain in the north, into Italy in the south, into Greece and Turkey in the east; and from about 450 B.C. to 250 B.C. they were the most powerful people in Europe.

Historians are not certain when the Celts first came to Ireland, but it was probably about 600 B.C. They were not the first settlers, in fact, Ireland has been inhabited since about 6000 B.C., but they did change the pattern of life throughout the country. They brought in new customs and skills, especially the ability to make tools and weapons from iron, and introduced the distinctive Celtic language.

Ireland never formed part of the Roman Empire. The next wave of invaders, the Vikings, did not start raiding until the eighth century, so Celtic customs and the way of life survived relatively undisturbed even though Christianity was introduced in the fifth century.

Map showing the expansion of the Celts from their original homeland in central Europe.

BLACK SEA

MEDITERRANEAN SEA

*BONE FLAKE, one of hundreds discovered in
a megalithic tomb at Loughcrew, Oldcastle,
Their function is unknown and they have not been
found on any other site. While the tomb itself
dates to 2000 B.C. the ornament on the bone
flakes clearly indicate that they belong to Celtic
Ireland. The bone in the picture is about
10.16 cm. long and it dates to 1st century B.C.*

Reproduced from a woodcut made in Strasbourg in 1513
(from a manuscript in the National Library of Ireland.)

MAPS

Map making began in the Middle East, first with the Egyptians and then the Greeks. Ireland wasn't on the main trading routes, but would still have had contact with European countries. In the second century A.D., a Greek map maker called Claudius Ptolemy plotted the position of Ireland and collected information about the country. This map has been drawn from the information that Ptolemy gave in his writings.

THE COUNTRYSIDE

The Celtic invaders and settlers would have been faced with an Irish countryside much wilder and emptier than it is now. Large parts of the country were covered in forests and there were great areas of marshland and bog. Many places which are now bogland would then have been covered with trees, indeed men cutting turf often find remains of earlier settlements. As well as the forest and bogland there were large open plains where the people grew crops and grazed their animals, and plenty of rivers and lakes to supply fresh water.

Wild animals roamed freely through the countryside and there were numerous varieties of birds and fish. There were great herds of deer, wild boars with long and dangerous tusks, and even wolves in the woods. Flocks of cranes, wild geese and wild swans could be found in the lakes and marshlands, and kites, golden eagles and goshawks were much more numerous than they are now.

The Celts were a farming people and their homes were isolated rather than being grouped together in towns and villages. People could travel fairly easily from one place to another because there were plenty of rough roads and tracks, but if they didn't feel like walking they could go on horseback or in carts pulled by horses or oxen. Rivers were often difficult to cross, there would have been some wooden bridges or ferryboats, but people usually waded across at shallow fords. Causeways made out of layers of trees, brushwood, earth and stones were sometimes built across boggy land. People were expected to try and keep the roads in reasonable condition — an old Irish text stated:

'A road of whatever class must be cleared on at least three occasions, that is, the time of horse racing, winter and war.'

This is an old Irish poem written in the 7th century by a hermit living alone in a woodland. The countryside that he describes would not have changed much since the time of the earliest Celtic invaders.

THE HERMIT'S SONG

A hiding tuft, a green-barked yew tree
Is my roof,
While nearby a great oak keeps me
Tempest-proof.

I can pick my fruit from an apple
Like an inn,
Or can fill my fist where hazels
shut me in.

A clear well beside me offers
Best of drink,
And there grows a bed of cresses
Near its brink.

Pigs and goats, the friendliest neighbours,
Nestle near,
Wild swine come, or broods of badgers,
Grazing deer.

All the gentry of the county
Come to call!
And the foxes come behind them,
Best of all.

To what meals the woods invite me
All about!
There are water, herbs and cresses,
Salmon, trout.

A clutch of eggs, sweet mast and honey
Are my meat,
Heathberries and whortleberries
For a sweet.

All that one could ask for comfort
Round me grows,
There are hips and haws and strawberries,
Nuts and sloes.

And when the summer spreads its mantle
What a sight!
Marjoram and leeks and pignuts,
Juicy, bright.

Dainty redbreasts briskly forage
Every bush
Round and round my hut there flutter
Swallow, thrush.

Bees and beetles, music-makers,
Croon and strum;
Geese pass over, duck in autumn,
Dark streams hum.

Angry wren, officious linnet
And black-cap,
All industrious, and the woodpecker's
Sturdy tap.

From the sea the gulls and herons
Flutter in,
While in upland heather rises
The grey hen.

In the year's most brilliant weather
Heifers low
Through green fields, not driven nor beaten,
Tranquil, slow.

In wreathed boughs the wind is whispering,
Skies are blue,
Swans call, river water falling
Is calling too.

(Translated by Frank O'Connor)

APPEARANCE

The Celts seem to have been a rather striking people, tall, fair skinned and with fair or reddish hair. They were very concerned with their appearance and took special care of their hair which was usually worn fairly long. They were fond of jewellery and ornaments and the women probably used cosmetics; berry juice to dye their eyebrows and a herb called ruam to redden their cheeks. Personal hygiene was not neglected, there are references to people washing and bathing and using oils and sweet herbs to anoint their bodies after a bath.

There are several descriptions of the Celts by Roman historians; one of them called Strabo remarks that the Celts were figure conscious:

'...they try not to become stout and fat bellied, and any young man who exceeds the standard length of the girdle is fined.'

While another one, Diodorus Siculus gives us a very detailed picture. Diodorus was writing about the Celts who lived in the area now known as France. He called them Gauls, but his remarks apply to all the Celtic peoples.

'The Gauls are tall in stature and their flesh is very moist and white, while their hair is not only naturally blond, but they also use artificial means to increase this natural quality of colour. For they continually wash their hair with lime — wash and draw it back from their forehead to the crown and to the nape of the neck, with the result that their appearance resembles that of Satyrs or Pans, for the hair is so thickened by this treatment that it differs in no way from a horse's mane. Some shave off the beard, while others cultivate a short beard; the nobles shave the cheeks but let the moustache grow freely so that it covers the mouth. And so when they are eating the moustache becomes entangled in the food, and when they are drinking the drink passes, as it were, through a sort of strainer...'

The Celts were said to be great talkers and storytellers. Diodorus Siculus thought that they were boasters as well.

'Physically the Gauls are terrifying in appearance, with deep sounding and very harsh voices. In conversation they use few words and speak in riddles, for the most part hinting at things and leaving a great deal to be understood. They frequently exaggerate with the aim of extolling themselves and diminishing the status of others. They are boasters and threateners and given to bombastic self dramatization, and yet they are quick of mind and with good natural ability for learning.'

Hoard of gold objects found together by two ploughmen at Broighter, near Limavaddy, Co. Derry. Included are (top left) a beaten sheet gold bowl; three fine necklaces and a portion of a fourth; and a superb example of early Irish craftsmanship in the form of a hollow gold collar, the whole surface of which is decorated with raised designs. There is also a small boat complete with steering oar, fourteen rowing oars, seats for oarsmen and mast. The hoard dates to 1st century B.C.

In contrast to the rather fearsome picture painted by Diodorus, this is an eighth century Irish description of a handsome man.

Froech in the dark pool

...He went to come out of the water then. "Do not come out" said Ailill, "till you bring me a branch of that mountain ash on the bank of the river. Beautiful I think its berries". He went away then and broke a spray from the tree, and carried it on his back through the water. And this was what Findabhair used to say afterwards of any beautiful thing which she saw, that she thought it more beautiful to see Froech across the dark pool; the body so white and the hair so lovely, the face so shapely, the eye so blue, and he a tender youth without fault or blemish, with face narrow below and above, and he straight and spotless, and the branch with the red berries between the throat and the white face.

CLOTHING

The Celts wore simple, colourful clothes using the linen and woollen materials that they produced themselves. Men and women both wore tunics and long cloaks fastened with pins or brooches. Sometimes the men wore short, knee length trousers under their tunics as well. Shoes and sandals were made from leather and tied with thongs. Jewellery was very popular and rings, bracelets and torcs were worn by both men and women. A second century writer said:
'They wear ornaments of gold, torques on their necks, and bracelets on their arms and wrists, while people of high rank wear dyed garments besprinkled with gold.'
Archaeologists have found many of these pins, brooches and torcs and some of them can be seen in the National Museum in Dublin.

where
they lived

RING FORTS

HE CELTS did not live in towns or villages but in isolated farmsteads scattered throughout the country. These farmsteads are generally called forts, though they were not really designed for defence. The forts were mainly circular in design, and the land containing the house would have been surrounded by an earthen bank or stone wall and a ditch. Different Irish terms were used for the forts, those surrounded by an earth bank were commonly called raths, while the terms cathair and caiseal were used for those with stone walls.

Forts varied greatly in size, they were usually 40-50 metres in diameter, though some could be as much as 100 metres across. The surrounding bank of earth or stone would have been quite high, possibly even being topped with a wooden fence. There was only one entrance which was closed at night time. The dwelling house and storage buildings would have been inside the fort, and some of the land outside would have been cultivated. The animals would probably have been brought inside the fort at night to keep them safe from the attacks of wild animals and from thieves.

16

Lismore Fort, Co. Louth. The haystacks give an indication of the scale.

Underground passages or souterains have been found in some of the forts. Their exact purpose is uncertain, but they might have been used as a hide-out in times of danger or just as places for storing food.

The remains of these forts can be seen throughout the country and it has been estimated that there are between thirty and forty thousand — some country people still refer to them as fairy forts and regard them as magic places where humans are not really safe.

The Celtic nobleman or king would have had a much larger fort than the ordinary farmer. Not only would the house itself have been larger but more land would have been enclosed so that there would be space for sports and weapon training, as well as places for the animals. The king would have needed a strong fort that could be defended from his enemies and in which he could provide hospitality for his friends. In a royal fort someone would always have been on watch to guard the entrance and keep a look-out for visitors and troublemakers.

TOWNLAND NAMES

The remains of over thirty thousand Irish ring forts have been found. It would be difficult to reproduce a map showing their distribution. However it is possible to trace the ring forts from townland names since five terms were used to signify forts. These terms are dun, rath, lios, cathair and caiseal. The terms dun, rath, and lios are used for earthen banked forts, cathair and caiseal for stone banked ones. This map shows the distribution of forts by townland name.

*RING FORT. A ring fort built at Craggaunowen, Co. Clare. The
Craggaunowen project is an attempt to reconstruct dwellings similar to
those of the Celtic period.*

CRANNOGS

The forts were not the only type of dwelling in Ancient
Ireland, some people lived on crannogs which were artificial
islands that they made in the middle of the lakes or in bogs.
These islands were built up with layers of different materials,
usually peat and brushwood, but logs, stones, straw, rushes
and animal bones were also used. The crannog would then
have been fenced around with timbers, and extra ones would
have been driven into the foundations to hold the different
layers together.

The remains of over two hundred crannogs have been
found throughout the country, but only some of these sites
have been excavated, two of these are at Lough Gur and
Ballinderry Lough.

WINE STRAINER in the Roman manner. It consists of a small bronze bowl to which an iron handle is attached. The perforations form a pleasing pattern of three interlocking patterns. It dates from about 2nd or 3rd century A.D., and is from a crannog at Moylarg, Co. Antrim.

INSIDE A CRANNOG

Each crannog seems to have been the home of one family and their dependants rather than a group of families. The inhabitants were probably farmers whose land would be on the neighbouring shores of the lakes on which their dwellings were built. Pathways were sometimes built from the land out to the crannog, but boats were the chief means of transport and canoes made from hollowed-out tree trunks have been found in some of the sites. Because the crannogs tended to be rather damp the moisture in the ground has preserved many objects which completely decay under drier conditions and archaeologists have found wood and leather objects and even the remains of fabric. Objects that were used in the smelting of bronze and iron have also been discovered and it seems likely that the inhabitants of the crannog made all their own weapons and tools.

Right, above and below — This replica of a crannog has been built at Craggaunowen, near Quinn in Co. Clare. The reinforced fence, around the crannog (91.44 metres in circumference) was built with 4.57 metres high larch poles from the local forest and a total of 8,000 wattles. The circular house took 10.16 tonnes of mud to coat its wattle walls and 3,600 bales of rushes to thatch its roof. When the crannog was complete lake water was let in around it.

polítical organísation

ELTIC IRELAND was divided into about 150 tiny kingdoms called Tuatha and the people within each tuath were divided into four main groups, the king and his family, the nobles, the freemen and the unfree. Each tuath had its own king, who would lead the people into battle and represent them in peacetime, but he did not make the laws or act as judge. The nobles were land-owning families and warriors but druids, poets and some of the craftsmen also belonged to this group. The ordinary freemen were mainly farmers, and beneath them were the unfree people, slaves and bondsmen. A number of tuatha joined or allied together made up a local province which was ruled by a greater king. There would be kings for different provinces but there was no high king, or king of all Ireland. (Some kings afterwards began to claim this title, but not until the eighth century at earliest).

THE FAMILY GROUP

A family group was more important than any one individual in the tuath. In law the family group extended to four generations and included all the descendants of a common great-grandfather, this group was called the derbfine. Land was owned jointly by the group and they

22

23

would all have a share in any inheritance.

CHOOSING A KING

Although in theory any member of the royal derbfine could be king, the family chose the person best suited, one who could lead them in battle and manage their affairs in peacetime. There were two main conditions, the king was not to have any deformities or blemishes which might prevent him being a good warrior, or which might make the people laugh at him, and his father and grandfather must have been nobles. Though it was supposed to be a peaceful affair, rivals would often try to maim or kill each other to try and get the kingship for themselves.

THE KING

The king was a very important figure in Irish society, the ruler of his people in peacetime and their military leader in war. He was responsible for any contacts with other kings, either friendly or hostile, but he did not make the laws or usually act as judge. The people believed that the rule of a good king would make the tuath prosperous — the crops would grow well, the seas and rivers would be full of fish, men and animals would be fertile and there would be plenty of food. If the king was unjust there would be war and famine.

The king was often referred to in the laws, and in one instance even his activities were planned.

'There are seven occupations for a king; Sunday for drinking ale, for he is not a lawful chief who does not distribute ale every Sunday; Monday for judgement, for the adjustment of the people; Tuesday at chess; Wednesday seeing greyhounds coursing; Thursday at marriage duties; Friday at horse racing; Saturday at giving judgements.'

The following story from an old Irish manuscript, seems to suggest that only a foolish man would refuse to obey the king.

24

'Eating a mouse includes his tail.'

(Irish; author unknown, 9th – 10th Century).

...'That is true,' said the king, 'this is Lughaidh, and it is through fear of me that they do not name themselves'...

'Well now,' said the king, 'kill me a batch of mice.' Then he put a mouse in the food served to each man, raw and bloody, with the hair on, and this was set before them; and they were told they would be killed unless they ate the mice. They grew very pale at that. Never had a more distressing vexation been put upon them. 'How are they?' said the king. 'They are miserable, with their plates before them.' ... 'Tell them they shall be killed unless they eat.' 'Bad luck to him who decreed it,' said Lughaidh, putting the mouse in his mouth, while the king watched him. At that all the men put them in. There was one poor wretch of them who gagged as he put the tail of the mouse in his mouth. 'A sword across your throat.' said Lughaidh, 'eating a mouse includes its tail'. Then he swallowed the mouse's tail. 'They do as you tell them,' said the king from the door.

'I do as they tell me, too,' said Lughaidh.

'Are you Lughaidh?' said the king. 'That is my name' said Lughaidh...'

THE KING OF CONNACHT

(Translated by Frank O'Connor)

'Have you seen Hugh,
The Connacht King in the field?'
'All that we saw
was his shadow under his shield.'

HOSTAGE CHAIN beautifully made of graduated links with a decorated, hinged, iron collar. As Irish literature indicates, hostages were commonly given as a surety of good behaviour by one king or chieftain to another. This chain was found in the royal crannog of Lagore near Dunshaughlin, Co. Meath and dates to 7th century A.D.

SLAVES

Slaves were kept in some Celtic households, but they don't seem to have formed a large section of the population. They were mainly captives taken in battle and were probably kept as servants in noble households. They would have been given the heavy difficult work to do, ploughing, sowing and harrowing for the men and domestic duties for the women, especially corn grinding with the quern. Slave chains have been found in excavations and there seems to have been some trade in slaves. The Irish term for a female slave was cumal and her value was regarded as equivalent to three cows.

BRONZE TRUMPET, an example of excellent craftsmanship of the Celtic metal workers of Ireland. The two portions are each made of sheet metal folded over and secured along their edges by a strip of metal held on the inside by tiny rivets. It dates to 2nd century B.C. and was found in a dried up lake called Loughnashade just outside the bank of the Navan Rath near Armagh. About 2 metres long.

THE LAWS

The old Irish laws are called the Brehon Laws. They were not public laws passed in a parliament and enforced in the courts. They were the records of the old customs of the society, which were handed down orally by the poets and were only finally written down about the seventh century. We cannot know how effective these laws were in practice.

Fasting seems to have been one of the main ways of obtaining justice. A man who had a grievance in law against another would go and fast outside the defendant's house. If the defendant ignored him and refused to pay up he lost his honour. Fasting could also be used to bring some evil on a person, or as a sort of compulsion like a geis, to obtain a request from another.

The laws stated that compensation had to be made for any injury done. This compensation was related to the seriousness of the incident and also to the social rank of the person involved, it was called honour price. A chieftain had a higher honour price than a slave.

home life

HOUSES

WELLING HOUSES WERE built inside the fort and were usually circular in design. The walls of these houses were made of stone or wood, the roof supported on wooden poles and probably thatched with straw, reeds or rushes. The floor would have been of earth covered with straw or rushes, though if it became very messy extra clay might be brought into the house and a new surface put down on top of the old one. The fire would usually have been built in the centre of the room with a hole left in the roof through which the smoke would escape.

There were no separate rooms, and bedding would just have been spread around the walls at night, though in richer homes there might have been some partitions or screens to give some privacy. People slept on piles of straw and rushes covered with rugs and skins, the hairier the better. There would have been little furniture apart from a few wooden trestles and stools and cooking utensils.

WASHING AND BATHING

All the evidence that we have from the stories indicates that the Celts were particular about their appearance and washed frequently. It was expected that a host would offer visitors a bath, in fact it was probably very necessary if they had walked along muddy roads to reach him. Large

wooden bath tubs were used and the water would have been heated by throwing in hot stones. If several people were waiting for a bath they would probably have to use the same water. Ash made by burning bracken and briars was made into cakes and used as a soap.

FOSTERAGE

Fosterage was an important aspect of Irish life. Instead of keeping a child at home a man would often send a son or daughter to be brought up with another family. In this way the child would acquire a foster father and mother, and probably foster brothers and sisters. The children might be sent to fosterage at one year of age, and stay until they were considered old enough to marry, seventeen for a boy and fourteen for a girl. Sometimes children would be fostered without payment, but often some type of fee was involved. This fee was paid in land or more usually in cattle and varied according to rank. For the son of the lowest order of chief the fee was three cows, while for a king's son it might be as many as thirty. Higher fees had to be paid for the fosterage of girls because they were regarded as being more troublesome. A man was expected to care for his foster children as if they were his own family and to educate them for their place in life, in return the children were expected to help and support their fosterparents in difficult times.

The children of noble families would be carefully taught, the boys educated in riding, swimming and the use of weapons, the girls in sewing and embroidery. Children of lesser rank would be taught to work on the land and in the house, herding and farmwork for boys, the quern and kneading for girls.

These extracts from the old Irish laws show some of the regulations about fosterage:

'How many kinds of fosterage are there? Two: fosterage for affection and fosterage for payment. The price of fosterage of the son of a chief is three sets; four sets is the price of fosterage of his daughter' (A 'set' was half the value of a milch cow). 'There are three periods at which fosterage ends: Death, Crime and Marriage'.

ROLE OF WOMEN

Women had a very important role in Celtic society, and played an active part in everyday affairs. They had legal rights, and rights to own and inherit property. Women accompanied their husbands into battle and in some cases even joined in the fighting. Some were as skilled in the handling of weapons as men, and indeed Cuchulainn was trained as a warrior by two women – Skatha and Aife. There are descriptions of some of these fierce women in the literature. This one is by Ammianus Marcellinus, another Roman historian.

'Almost all the Gauls are of tall stature, fair and ruddy, terrible for the fierceness of their eyes, fond of quarrelling, and of overbearing insolence. In fact a whole band of foreigners will be unable to cope with one of them in a fight, if he calls in his wife, stronger than he by far and with flashing eyes; least of all when she swells her neck and gnashes her teeth, and poising her huge white arms, begins to rain blows mingled with kicks like shots discharged by the twisted cords of a catapult'.

The Celts had liberal views about marriage. Though it was the general custom to have only one wife, there were exceptions, and a man could have a chief wife and a second wife. If a couple did not suit each other, they could get a divorce without difficulty, by mutual consent, and there is some evidence that couples sometimes got married just for a year.

Extract from the laws:

'What are the marriageable ages?
At the end of fourteen years for the daughter and
at the end of seventeen years for the son'.

SAFETY PIN BROOCH seen from the back; it is made of cast bronze and was found at Navan Rath, Armagh. Date: 1st century B.C.

THE OLD WOMAN OF BEARE

The sea crawls from the shore
Leaving there
The despicable weed,
A corpse's hair.
In me,
The desolate withdrawing sea.

The Old Woman of Beare am I
Who once was beautiful.
Now all I know is how to die
I'll do it well.

Look at my skin
Stretched tight on the bone.
Where kings have pressed their lips,
The pain, the pain.

I don't hate the men
Who swore the truth was in their lies.
One thing alone I hate –
Women's eyes.

The young sun
Gives its youth to everyone,
Touching everything with gold.
In me, the cold.

The cold, Yet still a seed
Burns there.
Women love only money now.
But when
I loved, I loved
Young men.

Young men whose horses galloped
On many an open plain
Beating lightning from the ground
I loved such men.

And still the sea
Rears and plunges into me,
Shoving, rolling through my head
Images of the drifting dead.

A soldier cries
Pitifully about his plight;
A king fades
Into the shivering night.

Does not every season prove
That the acorn hits the ground?
Have I not known enough of love
To know it's lost as soon as found?

I drank my fill of wine with kings,
their eyes fixed on my hair.
Now among the stinking hags
I chew the cud of prayer.

Time was the sea
Brought kings as slaves to me.
Now I near the face of God
And the crab crawls through my blood.

I loved the wine
That thrilled me to my fingertips;
Now the mean wind
Stitches salt into my lips.

The coward sea
Slouches away from me.
Fear brings back the tide
That made me stretch at the side
Of him who'd take me briefly for his bride.

The sea grows smaller, smaller now.
Farther, farther it goes
Leaving me here where the foam dries
On the deserted land,
Dry as my shrunken thighs,
As the tongue that presses my lips,
As the veins that break through my hands.

(Translated by Brendan Kennelly)

Edain the Fairy
(Irish; author unknown; 9th century original)

'. . . He saw a woman at the edge of the spring, with a bright silver comb ornamented with gold, washing her hair in a silver bowl with four golden birds on it, and little flashing jewels of purple carbuncle on the rims of the bowl. She had a shaggy purple cloak made of fine fleece, and silver brooches of filigree work decorated with handsome gold, in the cloak; a long-hooded tunic on her, stiff and smooth, of green silk with embroidery of red gold. Wonderful ornaments of gold and silver with twining animal designs, in the tunic on her breast and her shoulder-blades on both sides. The sun was shining on her, so that the men could plainly see the glistening of the gold in the sunlight amid the green silk. There were two golden-yellow tresses on her head; each one was braided of four plaits with a bead at the end of each plait. The colour of her hair seemed to them like the flower of the water-flag in summer, or like red gold that has been polished.

She was loosening her hair to wash it, and her arms were out through the opening at the neck of her dress. Her upper arms were as white as the snow of a single night, and they were soft and straight; and her clear and lovely cheeks were as red as the foxglove of the moor. Her eyebrows were as black as a beetle's wing; her teeth were like a shower of pearls in her head; her eyes were as blue as the bugloss; her lips were as red as vermilion; her shoulders were high and smooth and soft and white; her fingers were pure white and long; her arms were long; her slender long yielding smooth side, soft as wool, was as white as the foam of the wave. Her thighs were warm and glossy, sleek and white. Round and small, firm and white, were her knees. Her shins were short, white and straight. Her heels were even and straight and lovely from behind. If a ruler were laid against her feet, it would be hard to find any fault with them, unless it should make the flesh or skin swell out on them. The bright blush of the moon was in her noble face; the lifting of pride in her smooth brows; the ray of love-making in both her royal eyes; a dimple of sport in both her cheeks, in which there came and went flushes of fast purple as red as the blood of a calf, and others of the bright whiteness of snow. A gentle womanly dignity in her voice; a steady stately walk, a queenly pace. She was the fairest and loveliest and most perfect of the women of the world that the eyes of men had ever seen; they thought she must be of the fairies...'

JEALOUSY	A LOVE SONG
Love like heat and cold	*Such a heart!*
Pierces and then is gone,	*Should he leave, how I'd miss him,*
Jealousy when it strikes	*Jewel, acorn, youth.*
Sticks in the marrowbone	*Kiss him!*
(Translated by Frank O'Connor)	*(Translated by Brendan Kennelly)*

HOSPITALITY

The Celts seem to have been very friendly and generous, not likely to turn a visitor away from the door. Strangers would be given food and drink before they were asked their business. Any man who failed to do this would be dishonoured and disgraced. Any special occasion like the return of a hero or a victory in battle was celebrated with a great party or feast. Even ordinary evenings would often be spent eating and drinking while listening to singers and storytellers.

FEASTING

A feast was an occasion for great celebration and rejoicing, though it could often end in bloodshed as well if a hero thought that he wasn't being treated with enough honour and attention. Men and women usually sat round in a circle at a feast, taking their places according to rank and giving the most important or influential man the senior position. The champion warrior was given the best portion of meat, and fights often took place to decide who should receive this. Particular joints of meat were reserved for certain individuals at a feast, e.g. a leg of pork for a king, a haunch for a queen, a boar's head for a charioteer.

Posidonius, a writer who was working between 135 B.C. and 51 B.C. gave this description of Celtic feasts:

'The Celts sit on dried grass and have their meals served on wooden tables raised slightly above the earth. Their food consists of a small number of loaves of bread together with a large amount of meat, either boiled or roasted on charcoal or on spits. They partake of this in a cleanly but leonine fashion, raising up whole limbs in both hands and cutting off the meat, while any part which is hard to tear off they cut through with a small dagger which hangs attached to their sword sheath in its own scabbard... When a large number dine together they sit around in a circle with the most influential man in the centre, ... Beside him sits the host and next on either side the others in order of distinction.... The drink of the wealthy classes is wine imported from Italy or from the territory of Marseilles... The lower classes drink wheaten beer prepared with honey, but most people drink it plain... They use a common cup, drinking a little at a time, not more than a mouthful, but they do it rather frequently'.

OISIN

The teeth you see up here,
Up in the ancient skull,
Once cracked yellow nuts
And tore the haunch of a bull.

Savage and sharp and huge,
Crunching the naked bone,
Every tittle and joint
Was mince when they were done.

The eyes you see up here,
Up in the aged skull,
Dull they may seem tonight
But once they were never dull.

Never in darkest night
Did they take trip or fall;
Now though you stand so close,
I cannot see you at all.

The legs you see below,
Nothing could weary them then;
Now they totter and ache,
A bundle of bones and skin.

Though now they run no more,
All their glory gone,
Once they were quick to follow
The shadow of golden Fionn.

(Translated by Frank O'Connor)

STONE CUP, carved out of a single piece of soap stone, it measures 20.32 cm. across and was found at Ballinenagh, Co. Tipperary.

LARGE CAULDRON *made of thin bronze plates riveted together. This is the sort of vessel frequently referred to in early Irish literature and it could have been used for boiling meat. From Lack East, Co. Clare, it dates to about the 5th century B.C. Breadth about 52 cms.*

FOOD

Milk, cheese and meat formed the main part of the Celtic diet. Bread does not seem to have been eaten in large quantities, but corn was used to make a variety of porridges. Cattle were kept for their milk rather than their meat, and though beef was eaten the animals slaughtered for this purpose would be old or maimed ones or unwanted bull calves. Pork was very popular and seems to have been the main meat eaten at feasts, but mutton and venison were eaten as well.

Milk was an important foodstuff and was consumed in large quantities; it might be drunk fresh, allowed to go sour and eaten as curds, or used to make a variety of cheeses and butter. Porridge was made in many different ways, using grain from oats, barley or wheat. It was mixed with fresh or sour milk, flavoured with honey, salt or herbs, made very thick or almost liquid and could be eaten hot or cold.

Fish were caught in the rivers and lakes and cooked over the fire. The salmon was the most prized of all fish, but trout, sea fish and shell fish were all eaten as well.

There is little evidence in the literature about the vegetables that were eaten, and people probably relied on those that they could gather in the wild rather than growing them themselves. They probably used onions, wild leeks, sorrel, nettles, and watercress. A variety of fruits could have been gathered in the summer, sloe, wild cherry, raspberry, blackberry, strawberry, rowan, crabapple and elderberries, but apples seem to have been the only fruit that was cultivated in any way.

Though the winter months were probably hard, the Celts generally seem to have eaten well. Certainly they do not seem to have wasted food; an old Irish text says:

'Anyone who gives another anything in which there has been a dead mouse or dead weasel, three fasts are laid on him who gives it.. If it is in any other dry food, in porridge or in thickened milk, the part round it is thrown away, the rest is consumed'.

The seating plan of the banqueting hall at Tara, from an ancient manuscript.

	Distributors (or dividers):—a *mael* for them.	Cupbearers:—a *mael* for them	Herdsmen:—a *mael* for them.	Charioteers:—crooked bones for them.
…emen, or charioteers, and …ards:—*cuinn* for them.				Steward:—*cuind* for him.
…ers and timpanists:—a shoulder for them.	Pipers:—a *colptha* for them.	Fire.	Chess-players:—a *colptha* for them.	Hunters:—a pig's shoulder for them.
…ons:—a *lon-chroichti* for …	Scolaige:—a *less-croichte* for them.	Fire.	Drink-bearers:—a *les-chroichti* for them.	*Aire forgill*:—a *lon-chroichte* for them.
…essor of Literature:—a *lon-chti*. Tanist professor:—a …ochait or *prim-chrochait*.	Artisans:—an *ir-croichte* for them.		Braziers:—an *ir-croichti* for them. Fools:—an *ir-croichti* for them.	*Ruiri*:—a *lon-croichte* for them. Queen and royal *ruireach*:—a *les-croichte* [for them].
…m poet:—a *loarcc* for him. …udh [poet]:—a crooked bone.	Smiths:—a *mael* for them.	Fire. Vat.	Physicians and mariners:—a *mael* for them.	*Aire ard*:—a *loarc* for them. *Cli* [poets]:—a crooked bone for them.
…gu and *aire tuisi*:—a *laracc* …hem.	Shield-makers:—a *milgit-ain* for them.		Mariners:—a *milgitain* for them.	*Aire tuisi*:—a crooked bone. Historian:—a *loarc* for him.
…tarsair:—a pig's shoulder. …tanist:—a crooked bone.	Chariot-makers:—a *mil-gitain* for them.	Candle.	*Creacoire*:—crooked bones for them, or pig's *colptha*.	*Aire desa*:—a *colptha* for them. *Dos* [poet]:—a pig's shoulder. Or thus: Carpenters and *airig echta*.
…urs, druids, and *comail*:—*Ilptha* for them.	Jugglers:—a pig's *colptha* for them.		Buffoons:—a pig's *colptha* for them.	*Fochloc* [poet]:—an *ir-croichte* for him. Or: *aire desa*.
…se-builder, carpenter, and …churan, and rath-builder:—*r-croichti* for them.	Satirists:—the fat [part of the] shoulder for them.	Lamp.	*Braigtoire*:—the fat [part of the] shoulder for them.	Cooks, and *creccoire* or *cornaire*:—*midh mir*.
…npeters, and footmen, or …se-builders:—cheering …d for them.				Rath-builder and *oblaire*:—a *milgitain* for them.
		Common Hall.		*Aire echta*:—a pig's shoulder. *Canu* [poet]:—a crooked bone.
…ravers and ring-makers:—*ilgatan* for them.				
…e-makers and turners:—the [part of the] shoulder for …n.	The King's doorkeepers:—and chines for them.		The King's fools:—backs for them.	*Muirighi*, and *clasaighi*:—the fat [part of the] shoulder.
		Door.		

COOKING

The main way of cooking food was over the open fire; archaeologists have not found remains of ovens in the house sites. Meat was roasted on a spit over the fire, or made into a stew in a cauldron. Bread could be put to bake on a hot flagstone in front of the hearth. However the iron or bronze cooking cauldrons would have been valuable possessions, not easily available, so other methods of preparing food were devised. Remains of ancient cooking places show that hot stones were used to heat water, and roast meat. A wooden trough would be filled with water which was brought to the boil by adding stones which had been heated in the fire, meat could then be put in to cook.

A cooking trough like this was discovered in a bog at Ballyvourney in Co. Cork. It held 500 litres of water and the archaeologists found that this amount could be brought to the boil in thirty minutes by adding stones. Once the water was boiling they only had to add another stone at intervals to keep up the temperature. They cooked a leg of mutton perfectly by wrapping it in straw and then boiling it for 3½ hours in this trough. Meat could be roasted by placing the joint on a hot stone and covering it with a mound of hot stones.

Once prepared the food would have been served simply, possibly in a common bowl or dish. Drinking vessels and bowls were usually made from wood which was easily obtainable rather than metal. Wicker baskets could have been used to contain food as well.

The laws suggested the type of food that children should be given when they were being fostered:

'Stirabout is given to them all; but the flavouring which goes into it is different. Salt butter for the sons of inferior grades, fresh butter for the sons of chieftains and honey for the sons of kings. The food of them all is alike, until the end of the year or three years i.e. salt butter, and afterwards fresh butter to the sons of chieftains and honey to the sons of kings'.

'Stirabout made of oatmeal or buttermilk or water is given

BRONZE BOAR – *a wonderful example of the metal workers art, this piece dates from about 200 B.C. It measures about 7.62 cm. in length.*

to the sons of the Feini grades, and a bare self sufficiency of it merely, and salt butter for flavouring. Stirabout made on new milk is given to the sons of the chieftain grades and fresh butter for flavouring, and a full sufficiency of it is given to them and barley meal upon it. Stirabout made on new milk is given to the sons of kings, and wheaten meal upon it and honey for flavouring'.

The story of Mac Datho's Pig

Mac Datho was a lord of Leinster and his fort was one of the five chief hostels in Ireland. The others were — the hostel of Da Derga at Donnybrook, near Dublin; Forgall Monach beside Lusk; Da Res in Breffni and Da Choga in West Meath. Each hostel had seven doors: seven roads led to it; there were seven hearths and seven cauldrons on each hearth.

An ox and a salted pig went into each cauldron. The traveller who came to the hostel was told to thrust the flesh fork into the cauldron. Whatever came up at the first thrust, that was the share. If nothing came up at the first thrust the wayfarer went hungry.

Mac Datho was a very hospitable man so he was well fitted to be in charge of a hostel. He had a famous hound, called Ailbe, which could run all round Leinster in a day and a boar which was the largest in the world.

One day a messenger came from Queen Maeve of Connaught, asking Mac Datho to sell the hound. Maeve offered six hundred milch cows, a chariot with two of the best horses in Connaught and, at the end of the year as much again.

'That is a good offer!' said Mac Datho politely. But he was fond of the hound and did not want to part with it. As he sat considering, another messenger arrived — this time from King Conor of Ulster. And he brought an offer for the hound.

'Conor of Ulster offers as much as Maeve of Connaught and as well, the friendship and alliance of Ulster'.

'That is also a good offer!' said Mac Datho.

But still he could not bear to part with his hound. For three days he did not eat while he thought and thought what he should do. At night he could not sleep for grieving over the loss of Ailbe and the fear that whatever he did, worse would happen. And he did not know who to ask for advice.

His wife was sorry for him.

'What ails you?' she asked. 'You won't eat the good food that's put before you and you spend the night tossing and turning instead of sleeping'.

'There's a saying' said Mac Datho crossly, 'never trust a slave with money, nor a woman with a secret'.

'You're not getting much comfort from your wisdom!' retorted his wife. 'I might be able to settle your trouble'.

Mac Datho had never known her to give foolish counsel, so he told her the whole story.

'You see the fix I'm in? Which ever one I refuse, will take my cattle and slay my people!'

'That's not so easily settled,' agreed Mac Datho's wife. 'Whatever you do, you can't keep the hound – that's for sure! So give it to both of them and say they must come and fetch it. If there is any fighting to be done, let them fight each other. It's the best advice I can give you and bad's the best!'

Mac Datho thought it good advice and obeyed his wife. He sent for Queen Maeve's messenger and said to him –

'It's taken me a long time to make up my mind. Now I've decided to give the hound to Connaught. But Maeve and her husband, Ailill, must come themselves with their warriors and servants to bring it away and I'll have a feast prepared, worthy of them'.

The messenger rode off delighted, thinking how pleased Maeve and Ailill would be when they heard the news.

The moment he was out of the gate, Mac Datho sent for the Ulster messenger. 'It hasn't been easy for me to agree to give up my hound,' he told him. 'But at long last I see there's nothing else for it. Tell Conor he will be welcome here to the best feast the country has known and let him bring with him his friends and fighting men'.

Away went the Ulster man to King Conor and Mac Datho ordered the feast.

The great boar was killed and roasted: cakes made with

44

nuts and honey, stewed meat and soup thickened with herbs, drink of all kinds was laid upon the tables and as the boar was carried into the hall on a shield, the guests marched in.

Conor was surprised to see Maeve and Ailill: they were even more surprised to see him. The Ulstermen and the Connaughtmen sat at different tables. But Conor, Maeve and Ailill sat with Mac Datho at the high table.

Before the feast could begin, the boar had to be carved.

'That is a fine boar!' agreed Ailill. 'How shall it be divided Mac Datho?'

Before the host could answer, Briccriu, whose great pleasure was in making quarrels, leaned forward.

'Isn't it the custom that the bravest man in the company should carve the boar?' he asked. 'All the best warriors of Ireland are here. It should be easy to decide who is the finest fighter!'

'That is a sensible arrangement!' declared Ailill.

'There are many of our Ulster lads here who have fought all through the country,' said Conor. 'It should not be hard to choose the best man'.

Along the tables the warriors shouted the brave deeds they had done. Ulstermen glared at Connaughtmen. The spears and swords still leaned against the walls below the shields, but Mac Datho knew it would not be long before they were taken up and used.

At last Ket, one of the Connaughtmen, leaped from his seat and, standing over the boar, knife in hand, challenged each of the Ulstermen to match his brave deeds. One after another, they told their best fights and with every one of them Ket had a braver story to tell. He looked about him triumphantly and was about to carve the boar, when a roar of welcome came from the Ulstermen seated at the end door and in strode Conall of the Victories. He strode up to the boar and Conor, who had been frowning, smiled again.

'I see the feast is ready,' said Conall. 'Who is carving the boar?'

'Ket,' they told him, 'for he is the bravest here!'

'Is that so?' asked Conall.

'It is!' replied Ket. 'And you are welcome to the feast, victorious Conall!'

Conall stood before him.

'And now step away from the boar that I may carve it!' he said.

'Why should I do that?' demanded Ket.

'Because since I first took weapons in my hand I have never passed one day that I did not kill a Connaughtman, nor one night when I did not make a foray on them'.

Ket bent his head.

'You are then a better man than I am' he said. 'Take my place by the boar. But if Aluain, my brother were here, he would match every deed of your with a better, and it is a sorrow and a shame that he is not!'

'Aluain is here!' shouted Conall, and drawing from a bag the head of Aluain he flung it at Ket.

Every man in the hostel sprang to his feet, seized spear or sword and attacked the nearest man in the hostile force. Out from the hall they swept, cutting and thrusting, until King Ailill sprang into his chariot and, with Maeve beside him, shouted to the Connaughtmen to stop the foolish fight and follow.

The Ulstermen pursued them. Ailbe, the hound, excited by the tumult, raced ahead and coming up with the chariot, caught the pole in its teeth. Ailill drew rein but the charioteer raised his sword and struck at the hound with a mighty blow, cutting off its head.

So neither Connaught nor Ulster won the hound and, though Mac Datho lost it, he saved his lands and his people.

from 'Tales of Enchantment' by Patricia Lynch
(Clonmore and Reynolds)

A Fishing Harpoon

46

CARING FOR THE SICK

It was a well established tradition among the Celts to care for those who were sick. According to law a person who had wounded another had to take the victim into his own house and look after him till he recovered. Though he didn't have to do this till a few days after the incident:

'Not removed before the ninth day is any person transfixed by a spear or any invalid of whom it is not known whether he will live or die. For it is wasted labour if anyone maintain a doomed person'.

Certain people were not entitled to sick maintenance:

'There are three men in the territory who have no right to either nursing or fines: A man who refuses hospitality to every class of person, a man who is false to his honour, a man who steals everybody's property – men who do not observe their just obligations'.

The laws stated how the sick were to be treated, and the food that they were to receive:

'Let there be proclaimed what things are forbidden in regard to him who is on his sick bed of pain. There are not admitted to him into the house fools or lunatics, or senseless people or half wits or enemies. No games are played in the house. No tidings are announced. No children are chastised. Neither women nor men exchange blows. No hides are beaten. There is no fighting. He is not suddenly awakened. No conversation is held across him or across his pillow. No dogs are set fighting in his presence or in his neighbourhood outside. No shout is raised. No pigs grunt. No brawls are made. No cry of victory is raised nor shout in playing games. No shout or scream is raised'.

'There are three condiments which the rule of nursing in Irish law excludes: Every salt fare which is prepared with sea produce, the flesh of a whale and of a horse, and honey. For the produce of the sea impels one to drink. Does not horse flesh stir up sickness in the stomach of wounded heroes? Stomachs endure not a storm save people who can retain it. It is not right to give horse flesh to any invalid. Honey disturbs the stomach in which there is looseness of the bowels'.

47

WORK

ORTS AND CRANNOGS were scattered widely throughout the country and as there were no towns or trading centres the people had to be largely self sufficient. Everything that they needed, food, shelter, clothing, tools, weapons etc. they would have to provide themselves. Celtic society was not very free, and much of the heavy menial work would have been done by slaves or those of lesser rank, nevertheless it seems unlikely that the chiefs spent as much time fighting and feasting as the stories might suggest.

CATTLE

The Celts owned great herds of cattle and these were their most valued possessions. Though the animals were kept mainly for their milk rather than their meat, they were one of the chief sources of food, and the whole way of life depended on them. A man's wealth and social standing was measured by the number of cattle that he owned, and prices, wages and marriage portions were all estimated in cows. Cattle raiding was common and was the start of many battles.

It seems likely that many of the animals were killed in the autumn and their meat salted and kept for later use, because grass was in short supply during the winter months. Nevertheless herding the cattle and protecting them from animals and thieves would have been a full time occupation. When a

*IRON AXE HEAD (above)
with portion of the wooden handle.
It is an example of one of the earliest
attempts of Irish blacksmiths to forge
iron. It was found in a crannog in
Lough Gara, Co. Sligo and dates to
about 200 B.C.
IRON SPEAR HEAD (below)
ornamented on the blade with inlaid
bronze rings, from Corofin, Co. Clare
it dates to first century B.C.*

cow was killed it not only provided beef for the household, but a hide which was used for everything from footwear to covering curraghs.

PIGS

Every farmer would have owned some pigs and large numbers of them roamed freely through the woodland, feeding on acorns and anything else that they could pick up. They were easy to manage because they could remain outdoors without shelter for most of the year. Pork seems to have been a most popular meat and it was always supplied at feasts.

These Celtic pigs seem to have been a very vicious breed. The reference to pigs in the stories and writings indicate that they were long snouted, thin, muscular and active, always ready to attack and able to scour the country like hounds.

A contemporary writer Diodorus Siculus said:

'Their pigs are allowed to run wild and are noted for their height, and pugnacity and swiftness. It is dangerous for a stranger to approach them, and also for a wolf'.

HUNTING AND TRAPPING

Hunting was a major sport and leisure time occupation, as well as being a necessity of life. It was the main means of providing extra meat for the home. Deer and wild boar were hunted when food was wanted, but if the men were just out for a day's sport they would chase foxes and hares, or even wolves and badgers. Huntsmen seem to have moved on foot more often than on horseback, but they would always have been accompanied by packs of dogs, usually wolfhounds if large dangerous animals were being chased.

Deer were often caught in elaborate traps as well as being hunted down. One common method was to dig a deep pit, place a trap at the bottom and then cover the entrance with brambles; the deer would step on it unawares and plunge down into the trap.

Birds were caught in a variety of ways, stolen out of nests or brought down in flight by a stone thrown from a sling. In

*DEER TRAP made from wood. Drawing from the original
in the National Museum of Ireland.*

*BRONZE FISH HOOK
— Three different views.
The loop is designed in
the style of an animal's head. It
is about 7.62 cm. high and was
found at Carrownanty, Co. Sligo.*

coastal areas men were sometimes lowered down a cliff face in a basket at the end of a rope, so that they could collect eggs and chicks from the nests.

FISHING

Fish provided a valuable addition to the diet and fishing was a common pursuit with those who had access to rivers, lakes or the sea. Salmon and eels were often caught with a trident spear, but hooks and lines and nets were used as well. A fishing net was often owned in common by the fine or family group of relations and any fish caught would be shared among the group.

MY STORY
(Translated by Brendan Kennelly from an early Irish poem)

Here's my story; the stag cries,
Winter snarls as summer dies.

The wind bullies the low sun
In poor light; the seas moan.

Shapeless bracken is turning red,
The wildgoose raises its desperate head.

Birds' wings freeze where fields are hoary.
The world is ice. That's my story.

WOODEN DUGOUT CANOE. These vessels, used mainly on inland waters, were carved out of a full split oak tree trunk. They were propelled with broad bladed wooden paddles held in two hands by a paddler seated on the bottom. They range in date from the Stone Age down to mediaeval times, and were used to transport people, animals and goods. This example is about 3.65 metres long.

*QUERN STONE. This is the upper
part of a Quern used about the
1st century A.D. for grinding corn.
Note the wooden handle (a modern
reconstruction) inserted into the
stone. This is an example of the
'bee-hive' type of Quern.*

BOATS

The countryside was thickly wooded, and roads often little more than rough tracks, so it must often have been easier to travel by water than on land. The two main types of boat that were used were the curragh and the dugout canoe. Curraghs are still used in the west of Ireland and they have changed little in design. They were made by stretching hides over a wooden frame and stitching them together with leather thongs. Sometimes two or three layers of hide were used to make the boats stronger and safer.

Dugout canoes were made in large numbers and seem to have been widely used on inland lakes and rivers. They would have provided the main means of communication between a crannog and the shore. Archaeologists have found the remains of many of these canoes varying in length from two to twenty metres. They were made from a single tree trunk, usually oak, and were roughly shaped at either end. The inside would either have been burnt out or chipped away with an axe. It seems that the bottom of the canoes was thicker than the sides; the extra weight would make them easier to right if they capsized.

USING THE QUERN

Much of the routine work about the house was done by the women. One of the main jobs was the preparation of food, often a slow task, especially as the corn used for bread and porridge had to be ground by hand. The small hand mills that were used for this purpose were called querns. They were quite simple in design, two stones the bottom one slightly convex in shape, the upper one concave, were fitted on top of each other, corn was poured in between them through a hole in the top stone, then a handle was fitted in position and pushed round so that the top stone moved over the bottom one. In this way the corn was ground into flour which fell out around the sides of the quern. This rotary quern was a Celtic innovation; in the earlier type called saddle querns, a round stone was merely pushed back and forth over a pile of grain placed in the bottom of a hollow stone. Though most of the grain used would have been ground by hand at home, it is probable that there were a few mills in use. The earliest type was a horizontal water mill, and in these a chute of water was directed against the wheel which turned the mill stones.

WEAVING

The woollen cloth used to make cloaks and tunics would have been woven in the home, usually by women. Simple looms were made from branches, and the strands of wool would have been weighted down with heavy stones. The fabrics would have been dyed with a variety of vegetable dyes and stains before they were made into garments as the Celts were fond of brightly coloured clothes. Saffron made a yellow dye for tunics, seaweeds and lichens could produce purple and reddish colours. Some of the clothes would probably have been embroidered by the women.

FIGHTING

The Celts were a proud, brave people, quick to defend their honour and warlike in spirit. Cattle raids or disputes about the ownership of land or possessions often resulted in great wars that could involve whole provinces. Kings were expected to be skilled at leading men in battle, and the Celtic heroes were always great warriors. Violence broke out easily as the young men trained to use weapons from their boyhood, were always eager to demonstrate their courage and fearlessness in conflict. A 2nd century writer said of the Celts:

'The whole race... is madly fond of war, high spirited and quick to battle.....'

SINGLE COMBAT

The practice of fighting in single combat was quite common and disputes were often settled in this way. Each side would choose their bravest warrior, and these two men would then fight each other to the death. Warriors were quick to fight if they thought that they had been insulted in any way.

'The Celts sometimes engage in single combat at dinner. Assembling in arms they engage in a mock battle drill, and mutual thrust and parry but sometimes wounds are inflicted and the irritation caused by this may lead even to the slaying of the opponent unless the bystanders hold them back'.

(Posidonius)

HEADHUNTING

One of the more unpleasant Celtic customs was to cut the heads off enemies that they had slain in battle. These heads were carried home as trophies, and then would often

56

be left as offerings to the gods.

WEAPONS

Swords and spears were the weapons most commonly used by the Celts, though slings, stones and battle axes were also available. Shields were usually used for protection and helmets and jerkins might have been worn as well, though there are several references in the literature to the Celtic warriors going naked into battle.

This comment was made by Diodorus Siculus:

'Some of them so far despise death that they descend to do battle, unclothed except for a girdle'.

The iron swords were fairly long and bent easily, it seems that they often became twisted after the first blow and had to be straightened with the foot. The spears had wooden shafts and metal heads and were widely used for hunting as well as fighting. The spear heads were either leaf shaped or shouldered. The shields were usually made of alder wood and covered in leather. They were round or rectangular and the hand grip in the centre was protected by an extra piece of wood called a boss.

Light two-wheeled chariots were used by warriors riding into battle. There was room for two men; a warrior and a charioteer. They would drive right up to the enemy, hurling spears at them, then the warrior would often jump down to fight in hand to hand combat, relying on the charioteer to come in and rescue him if he got into difficulties. The fear of invasion and attack was always present.

IRON SWORD with bronze hilt mounts. This is a typical sword of the Celtic people who lived in Ireland; it dates to 3rd century B.C. and was found at Cashel, Co. Sligo.

57

Leísure

THE ROUTINE OF working, hunting, possibly fighting would have occupied most of the day, but there is plenty of evidence to show that the Celts liked to enjoy themselves as well. Many everyday things could give great pleasure — a good day's hunting with the dogs, a house well thatched or a cloak well made, but above all the Celts seem to have loved an evening of eating and drinking, talking and singing. Feasts for special occasions could often last several days. Poetry and story-telling were an important part of Celtic life and evenings would be spent round a fire listening to the tales of kings and warriors, battles and triumphs. There were no written documents so the only way of learning about the past was to listen to the stories and poems and to try and remember them. Knowledge was passed on from one generation to another in this way.

POETS

A man had to study for many years to become a poet (file) because he had to learn all the traditional stories and poems by heart. However once he had done this he became a very respected man in society. The poets would travel around the country staying with different noble families, entertaining them and also bringing news of affairs in the rest of the country. They were protected by the laws and would have been well looked after though sometimes they were feared as much as respected. As well as telling the traditional stories and poems they would make up new ones, and people were often rather afraid that a poem would be made about them which would make them the laughing stock of the country.

A Roman writer Athenaeus made this reference to a poet:

'A Celtic poet who arrived too late met Louernius and composed a song magnifying his greatness and lamenting his own late arrival. Louernius was very pleased and asked for a bag of gold and threw it to the poet who ran beside his chariot. The poet picked it up and sang another song saying that the very tracks made by his chariot on the earth gave gold and largesse to mankind'.

THE BOORISH PATRON

I have heard that he does not give horses
for songs of praise;
he gives what is natural to him – a cow.

(Irish; author unknown; ninth century)

BRONZE OBJECTS, sometimes known as 'spoons' or 'castanets' their exact function is unknown. They are usually found in pairs, in Celtic countries, in graves of women. Date last century B.C.

GAMES

The Celts seem to have practiced a number of outdoor sports; running, jumping and ball games as well as a form of hurley. In addition gaming pieces and dice have been found and there are references to a board game using wooden pieces that were pegged into position. Two board games called brandub and fidchell were being played in Ireland about the 7th century A.D. and possibly much earlier.

MUSIC

The Celts loved music and no gathering or celebration would be complete without it. They realised how music can affect the feelings and emotions, and the stories often refer to the way musicians calmed individuals or lulled them into sleep.

Several different types of musical instrument were in use, though U-shaped lyres, harps and the timpan were probably the most common. (The timpan was a small stringed instrument played with a bow). Pipes and curved bronze trumpets were also in use – the trumpets were probably used on ceremonial occasions, to signal men in battle or to mark the arrival of an important individual for example. Music was often accompanied by singing and this would provide one of the main sources of entertainment.

OGHAM

The earliest writing in Ireland probably began about 300 A.D. It is called ogham after Ogmios, the Celtic god of writing and was not written on paper but carved onto stone and wood. The alphabet is made up of sets of up to five strokes on, diagonally across, or on either side of a central line – the central line being the edge of a stone. The inscriptions using the writing are carved on standing stones; they begin at the bottom and climb towards the top of the stone and, if necessary, continue down on the opposite side. These standing stones seem to have been used as gravestones and to mark the boundaries of land.

I
E
U
O
A
R
Z
NG
G
M
Q
C
T
D
H
N
S
F
L
B

An Ogham stone from Coolmagort and now at Dunloe, Co. Kerry.
Early Christian period. Key to Ogham writing (left).

Belief

HE CELTS BELIEVED that magic forces filled every aspect of their lives and surroundings. They thought that the gods were very powerful and tried to keep them in good humour by offering sacrifices. They had many gods and godesses, each one responsible for some aspect of their lives, and they also believed that woods and trees, wells and rivers were often sacred places. The chief god was Dagda, the good god and the father of the people, but there were many others. For example, Morrigan a fierce warrior goddess, and Lug the fertility god celebrated in the August festival, Lughnasa.

The Celts didn't build great temples to their gods, but used groves in the forest or the land beside a sacred pool for their religious ceremonies. Sometimes they carved statues to their gods out of stone or wood, but often they would just use a mishapen tree trunk as an image. Sacrifices were an important part of the religious ceremonies. Animals would be killed but there was probably occasional human sacrifice too.

The Celts believed that the soul did not die but lived on, and for this reason they do not seem to have been afraid of death. They did not think of their gods as remote beings living in a far off heaven, but as magic people who lived in a hill or underground and who could contact mortals if they wished. They believed in a wonderful supernatural world called Tir na nÓg – The Land of Youth. This was a marvellous place, peaceful, untroubled and very beautiful. A place where there was no disaster and no death and where everyone was happy. It was the home of gods but sometimes ordinary people could be taken away there; it would be so pleasant they wouldn't notice the days passing.

DRUIDS

The Druids were the priests of the Celtic religion. They were very learned men who were skilled in magic and they had a very important place in Celtic society. The Celts thought of the world as a magic place and relied on the Druids to advise them so that they would not anger the gods. The Druids would cast horoscopes and foretell the future and so help people to make decisions, even the kings listened to them. They would help to organise festivals and sacrifices and as well as this, they gave legal judgements. Because they were such learned men they were often called in to settle disputes between people, and to decide on rewards and punishments.

Many of the druids were famous teachers, and young noblemen would come to learn from them. A man could only become a druid after long years of study – possibly even as long as twenty years. There were no written documents so everything had to be learnt by heart. A druid would have to memorise all the traditional information and stories about the world, the history of the people, and the gods, so that he could then hand on this information to others.

Strabo the historian, writing in the first century, said of the Celts:

'They used to stab a human being whom they devoted to death in the back with a dagger and foretell the future from his convulsions'.

FESTIVALS

The Celtic year was divided into four parts according to the seasons, and the passage from one part to another was marked by a great festival. These festivals were:

Samain – Imbolc – Bealtaine – Lughnasa

Samain — celebrated on November 1st

Imbolc — celebrated on February 1st

Bealtaine — celebrated on May 1st

Lughnasa — celebrated on August 1st

They mainly had a religious significance though there was feasting and merrymaking as well. The festival of Samain was the most important as it marked the end of one year and the beginning of the next. The herds and flocks of animals would be gathered together before the winter, some would be spared for breeding purposes but the majority would be killed. The night before Samain, the time we now celebrate as Hallowe'en, was thought to be a magic time and people would make sacrifices to the gods, hoping to gain good fortune for the coming year. They were specially careful not to do anything that might anger the gods and so bring them misfortune.

The festival of Imbolc was held on February 1st. It was dedicated to the goddess Brigit and seemed to have been connected with the tending of sheep.

The festival of Bealtaine on May 1st was also very important. It marked the beginning of the warm season and the time when the cattle could be driven out to open grazing. Great fires would be lit throughout the country, and the druids would drive the cattle between two great fires to protect them against disease. Mayday has remained a time of celebration.

The festival of Lughnasa was celebrated on August 1st. Sacrifices were made to the god Lug to ensure the ripening of the crops and to gain a good harvest.

BURIALS

We are not exactly certain how the Celts buried their dead, since little evidence remains from this early Iron Age period in Ireland. Archaeologists have found a few examples of cases where the bodies had been cremated and the bones and ashes then buried and the area protected by a small circular ditch — these are called rim barrows. Sometimes a few possessions, jewellery or glass beads were placed beside the ashes. However whole skeletons have occasionally been found, proving that bodies were not always cremated. In addition there is evidence from Europe showing that the Celts also practised a form of chariot burial. Graves have been found where the warrior was laid on his back across the platform of his chariot with his weapons, shield and helmet by his side. Food, wine and fine vessels were often placed in the grave as well so that he could have a feast in the next life.

GEIS (plural 'gessa')

The word 'geis' means 'taboo' or 'prohibition'. Certain actions or objects were regarded as 'gessa', and to ignore them would bring misfortune or bad luck of some kind on the individual who did so. Usually 'gessa' were restrictions that applied to a particular person.

Examples

It was 'geis' for anyone to turn the left side of his chariot towards Emain Macha.

It was 'geis' for Cuchulainn to eat dog's flesh.

It was 'geis' for the King of Tara to be still in bed at sunrise in the plain of Tara.

It was 'geis' for Conaire whose father was a bird to hunt birds.

STONE HEAD. A view of a carved stone head found at Corravilla, Co. Cavan. It dates from the 2nd or 1st century B.C. and was most likely the head of a pagan god.

THE CHILDREN OF LIR

In the days when Ireland was inhabited by two races of people, the People of Dana or the De Danaan, and the Milesians, these two races agreed to divide the country between them so that they would no longer fight about territory.

They agreed that the Milesians would take the upper half, the half above the ground, and that the De Danaans would have the territory under the ground.

The De Danaans chose as their king Bov the Red, who was a very wise and noble man. All his subjects were loyal to him except Lir, the father of Manannan Mac Lir, the sea god. Lir was offended because he had not been chosen as king himself and from the day that Bov the Red became king, Lir avoided going to court and ignored him.

Some years later, Bov the Red sent for Lir and asked him if he would like to marry one of his three foster daughters. Bov hoped that this would give Lir a chance to forget his disappointment and become friendly once again. And indeed it did, Lir was so pleased to hear from Bov that he decided to set out immediately for the palace on the shores of Lough Derg.

Lir and his followers were given a great welcome when they arrived and a feast was prepared for them. The three foster daughters were present during the meal, and when everybody had eaten the king invited Lir to take his choice of the three girls. As all three were very beautiful it was not an easy decision, but eventually he decided to choose the eldest one, Eve.

Lir and Eve were married that same day and two weeks later Lir brought his bride home to Shee Finnehy.

After some time Eve gave birth to twins, a boy and a girl whom they called Aed and Finola. Lir loved his wife and children dearly and was very happy. Two years later, Eve gave birth to another pair of twins, two sons whom they named Fiacra and Conn. But sadly, Eve died soon after their birth. Lir was heartbroken at losing her, and he worried too about his children who were left without a mother.

Not long afterwards King Bov, who was sad to hear of Eve's death, sent a message to Lir asking him if he would like to marry Eva, the second foster daughter. Lir agreed, hoping that Eva would fill the empty place in the house.

So Lir went again to Bov's palace, married Eva and brought her back home with him. She looked after the children well and they loved her dearly in return. These children gave Lir great happiness, indeed he loved them so much that he liked them to sleep in a room near his own. Every morning when they awoke he played with them and told them stories. King Bov their grandfather was very fond of them too and they visited him frequently. They were beautiful and affectionate children, and everyone who knew them loved them.

Unfortunately, as time went on, Eva began to resent the care that was lavished on the children. She was jealous because Lir loved them so much and felt that even her father paid more attention to his grandchildren than to her, his own daughter. Slowly she began to hate the children till finally she could not bear to see them around the house and began to plan how she could be rid of them altogether. Finally her plans were made. One day she asked for her chariot to be brought round to the door and then called the children and told them that she was taking them to see their grandfather. So Aed, Finola, Fiacra and Conn got into the chariot with their stepmother and they set out on the journey.

They had only travelled a few miles from the palace when Eva stopped the chariot and tried to persuade her servants to kill the children. However, they were horrified at her wicked suggestion and refused to do as she asked, so they all journeyed on until they reached Lake Derravaragh in the middle of Ireland. Eva ordered everyone to get out of the chariot here, and she brought the four children down to the lakeside to bathe while the horses were resting. They went into the lake, and as soon as Eva saw that they were in the water she chanted a spell over them, and hit each of them with a druid's wand. Immediately Aed and Finola, Fiacra and Conn were changed into four beautiful white swans.

When they realised what had happened these four swans

looked sadly at their stepmother, and then Finola said 'Why have you done this to us Eva? We loved you, and we thought that you loved us. What did we do to deserve such a dreadful punishment?'

Eva forgot her jealousy as she suddenly realised what a terrible thing she had done, but it was too late to change the spell. The children had been condemned to a long exile, they had to spend three hundred years on Lake Derravaragh, three hundred years on the Sea of Moyle, and three hundred years on Inish Glora on the Western Sea. They would remain as swans until a prince from the north married a princess from the south, and until Christianity came to Ireland. Eva tried to lessen the suffering she had caused them by promising that though outwardly they would have a swan's shape, their personalities would be unchanged. They would still be able to talk and to make music. Then Eva got back into her chariot and continued her journey to her father's house. The four swans were left behind on the lake.

King Bov was surprised to see her arrive alone, especially when she said that Lir had not allowed the children to come with her, but he soon heard the true story. When he realised what had happened to his grandchildren he was heartbroken, and was determined that Eva should suffer for her evil deed. As a punishment he cast a spell over her and changed her into a demon spirit.

Afterwards Bov the Red, Lir and some of the nobles went to the shores of Lake Derravaragh. They made camp and settled there so that they could be near the swans and keep them company. In this way the next three hundred years on Lake Derravaragh passed pleasantly — the swans had friends around them, and were able to spend the days talking and making music — music so beautiful that it charmed everyone who heard it.

Finally however, the time came for them to move on to the Sea of Moyle. The four swans, Aed and Finola, Fiacra and Conn, were sad at this because they had been almost as happy on Lake Derravaragh as they had been as children at home, but they could not avoid the spell that had been placed on them.

Early one morning, having spoken to their father and friends for the last time, the swans sang a beautiful song in farewell, and then flew away from the lake, north towards the Sea of Moyle.

The four were depressed and miserable when they arrived on the Sea of Moyle. It was cold and stormy and the only company they had there were the shrieking sea-gulls and the seals. They missed their friends and they seldom talked or sang. They spent many lonely days and nights in this un-inhabited place, but at last the 300 years passed.

The time came to go to Inish Glora and the swans decided to visit Shee Finnehy, their father's home, on the way. It was so long since they had seen it, that they were really happy and excited as they flew south. But when they came near, and looked down they could not find any sign of Lir's palace. They searched everywhere for some trace but in vain. They walked on the hill where the palace had stood but they only found a few ruined walls, overgrown with nettles. They realised sadly that their old home had gone.

Next morning they continued their journey to Inish Glora and landed on a small lake there. It was a much more pleasant place than the Sea of Moyle, the climate was quite gentle and there were thousands of birds in the area – birds that gathered to listen to the swans when they were singing their sad songs.

By this time Christianity had come to Ireland. St. Patrick was travelling throughout the country preaching to the people and building churches and monasteries. One of his followers, a man called Kemoc, built a church on Inish Glora. One morning, soon after he arrived, the four children of Lir were woken up by the sound of the church bell. They were terrified because they had never heard anything like it before. Finola finally realised what it was and she was happy because it was one of the things that could break the spell that Eva had put on them so many years earlier. When she told the others this they began to sing with joy, and the sweet sound of their music reached Kemoc who was praying in his church on the far side of the lake. He went down to the shore and spoke to the swans, asking them if they really were the children of Lir, famous throughout the country for their singing. They told him that they were indeed these children, and he was able to say that the spell would soon be broken. He would look after them until it was removed. So the swans came ashore and went to Kemoc's house and lived with him there. He taught them about the teachings of Christ, they would join him in his prayers and the days passed happily.

However, a final thing was necessary before the spell could be broken — a princess from the south would have to marry a prince from the north. At this time Decca, daughter of Finmin, King of Munster, had just married Largen, King of Connaught. When Decca heard of the singing swans living on Inish Glora she was determined to capture them. She asked Largen to get the swans for her and he sent a message to Kemoc asking him to catch them. Kemoc refused. When the King heard this, he became very angry and went to Inish Glora himself to get the swans. He dragged them out of the little church where Kemoc had put them for safety. But he had only brought them a short way from the church door when their feathers dropped off and they became human again. Finola was a frail, white-faced old woman, and her three brothers were feeble old men, grey-haired, bony and wrinkled. When the King saw this he was very frightened and returned to his wife to tell her what had happened. The children of Lir asked Kemoc to baptize them because they felt they would die soon, and indeed they died peacefully a short time later. Kemoc buried them side by side in one grave, and he wrote their names on a tombstone over the grave —

"Aed, Finola, Fiacra and Conn — the Children of Lir"

the ulster cycle

Previous page —
WOODEN WHEEL— Found in a bog at
Doogarymore, Co. Roscommon, this
wooden block wheel dates from 400 B.C. It
was made in three pieces and held together
with long dowels. This type of wheel would
have been used on horse-drawn carts and chariots.

the
ulster
cycle

contents

WOODEN FIGURE Carved from a piece of pine, it probably has a religious meaning. It seems to have been mounted on a pillar. Found in a bog at Ralaghan, Co. Cavan, it dates to the last centuries B.C. and is about one metre high. Wooden figures are found on celtic sites in continental Europe, and in circumstances that suggest worship of spring wells or running water.

íntroduction

THESE TRADITIONAL STORIES provide one of our best sources of information about the life of the Celts in Ireland. Though they were not written down till at least the eighth century, they had existed for many hundreds of years before that. They formed part of the culture of the people and were remembered and handed down from one generation to the next. Bards and poets spent many years learning these tales and recounted them on their travels throughout the country.

There were special stories for each occasion, for example, marriages and deaths, but generally, the stories fit into four cycles or groups of tales.

THE MYTHOLOGICAL CYCLE contains stories about the gods and the spirit world.

THE ULSTER CYCLE tells about Ulster's great hero, Cuchulainn and the cattle raid into Ulster started by Queen Maeve of Connaught.

THE FENIAN CYCLE contains stories about the hero, Finn MacCool and his band of warriors called the Fianna.

Finally, there is the *HISTORICAL CYCLE* of stories about various kings.

The stories which follow are from The Ulster Cycle.

77

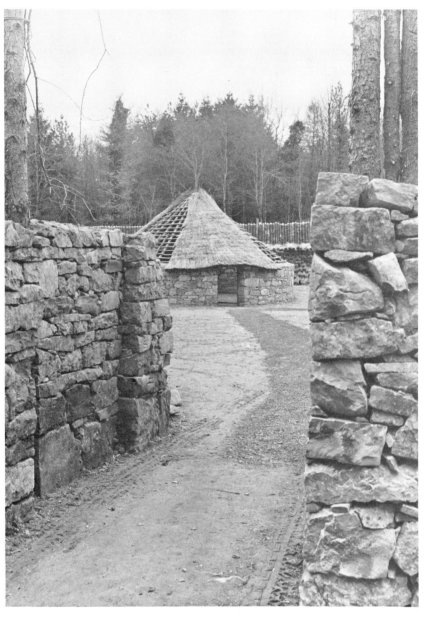

Replica of a crannog being built at Craggaunowen, near Quinn in Co. Clare.

how cuchulainn got his name

UCHULAINN WAS A great warrior and hero in the old days. He was not always called Cuchulainn, when he was a child he was called Setanta. His father was chieftain of Muirtheann, an area stretching from Dundalk in Co. Louth, southwards into Co. Meath. When he was seven years old he was sent away to be trained as a warrior (like many other young boys of his age). Even then he was unusual. When Setanta was young, there was a very famous sword-maker in Ulster called Culann the Smith. Culann earned his living by making swords. He did not own land or property and he was not as rich as the princes and chieftains. One day, Culann decided to have a feast. He invited King Conor, who was Setanta's foster father, and some of his followers as well. He didn't want too many people as he wasn't a rich man, so he asked Conor not to bring many followers with him. Conor decided to bring only fifty chariot-fulls of the highest and mightiest of his champions. This was considered a small number in those days.

On his way to Culann's feast, Conor visited the Boys' House where Setanta was at school. He saw Setanta in the playing fields playing ball against 150 boys and winning all the games. They were playing a game called Shoot-the-Goal. Setanta was able to get his ball into the goal even though

there were 150 boys against him. When it was the other boys' turn to shoot at the goal, Setanta defended the goal so well that not one ball got in. When they had finished playing this game it was time to wrestle. Setanta was better than all the rest at wrestling and he overthrew all 150 of them. But they could not throw Setanta even when they all tried together. King Conor was amazed when he saw all this. He realised that Setanta was a very strong boy and he decided to bring him to Culann's house in Ulster. He called Setanta out of the crowd in the playing field and said to him 'Will you come with me to the feast?' But Setanta didn't want to be disturbed from his games. 'I haven't finished playing yet,' he said, 'I'll follow you when I'm ready'.

Conor went ahead to Culann's house with his fifty chariots full of warriors. When they had all arrived Culann said to Conor: 'Is everybody here?' 'Yes' said Conor, forgetting that Setanta had said that he would follow. 'In that case,' said Culann, 'I will lock the gates and let my guard dog free to protect the house and my belongings. He's a very savage dog — it takes three chains to hold him, with three men on each chain'.

Soon afterwards, Setanta arrived at Culann's house. He had run all the way from the Boys' House, playing with his hurley and ball. He was tossing his ball and throwing his hurley after it and hitting it. Then he would throw his javelin after both the ball and the hurley and catch it before it fell. When he arrived at Culann's house, the dog raced towards him, but Setanta continued playing. From a safe distance in the house, Conor and his followers were watching. They realised that Setanta was in great danger. They were sure that the dog would kill him, but they were too far away to do anything to help. However, as the dog jumped to attack him, Setanta threw down the hurley, the ball and the javelin and tackled it with his two hands. He put one hand around the dog's throat and the other on his back. He lifted the dog and threw it against the nearest pillar with such strength that it was killed instantly.

When King Conor and his followers saw this they cheered and ran out and carried him shoulder high. They were delighted that Setanta, who was the son of the king's sister, had escaped. But Culann was not so happy. Although he was glad that Setanta had not been killed, he was very sad that his great guard dog was dead. 'My life is empty and my household defenceless now that I have lost my dog. He protected and sheltered our belongings and animals — we are lost without him' he said.

'I will be your hound' said Setanta. 'Until I have reared you a new pup from the same pack I will protect you and your possessions. I will be your dog'.

'Then we will call you Cuchulainn, the Hound of Culann' said Fergus McRoy, one of the King's followers. And they carried the boy into the house shouting his new name after him: 'Cuchulainn', 'Cuchulainn' and from that day on everybody called him Cuchulainn.

SPEAR BUTT. Cast in bronze, this is the butt (or ferrule) of a spear. The shaft would probably have been made of ash and the head of iron. This butt dates from the 2nd century B.C. and was found in the site of a crannog at Lisnacrogher, Co. Antrim. 6.75 cms. in length.

Deíntear laoch de chúchulainn

FTER CUCHULAINN HAD killed Culann's savage dog he went back to the Boy's House to finish his training there. One day he was in the woods with some of the other boys. They were sitting talking to Cathbad, one of their teachers. Cathbad was King Conor's father and he was also a druid — a wise man with some magic powers. While they were chatting, the boys asked Cathbad to use his magic powers to find out what it would be lucky to do on that day. At first Cathbad wouldn't tell them anything, but at last he said that anyone who took arms on that day would become famous. That person would be a strong and mighty warrior and stories about him would last forever. (When it was felt that a young man was ready to become a warrior he was given weapons for the first time. This was a special occasion and was remembered as the day when he had taken up arms).

When Cuchulainn heard what Cathbad had said, he decided that he would try to take arms immediately. He went to King Conor and said: 'I want to take up my weapons today. I have learned everything that is taught in the Boys' House. I am ready to become a warrior'.

Conor looked at him carefully and then slowly shook his head. Cuchulainn was small for his age, and didn't look at all like a warrior.

84

You're still very small,' said Conor 'a bit more height and a bit more strength would be a help'. Cuchulainn blushed. 'Size is not everything. If you lend me your hunting spears I'll show you how strong I am'.

Conor gave him two hunting spears. Cuchulainn took them and broke them across his knee as if they were twigs. 'Have you no better spears than this?' he asked. King Conor then gave him two war spears. Again Cuchulainn broke them easily and threw the broken pieces into the air.

By now there was a crowd watching. Cuchulainn stood in the middle waiting for someone to bring him better weapons. They brought him more spears and then swords but he broke them all. Then they brought him chariots but none of the chariots were strong enough for him – he broke them as easily as he had broken the spears.

At last King Conor decided to put an end to this. He brought out his own best battle spears and swords and chariot. Cuchulainn took the spears and swords and tried to break them across his knee, but he failed.

'Since you can't break them,' said the king, 'you can keep them. No other weapons are strong enough for you. Now, try the chariot'. Cuchulainn jumped up on the chariot but he couldn't smash the floor with his feet nor could he break the frame with his strong hands. So he took the reins, stood up in the chariot and sent the horses galloping. The king was amazed when he saw Cuchulainn controlling the horses so well. Nobody except the king's own charioteers had ever managed to control them before. After galloping around for a while, Cuchulainn led the horses back to the king and Conor said to him:

'You can keep my chariot and my horses. You are certainly a great warrior. Now you must leave the Boys' House'.

And so Cuchulainn became a warrior on that day. As Cathbad had predicted, Cuchulainn became famous. He was known ever afterwards as a strong and mighty hero and stories about him and his great deeds have lasted to the present day.

DEINTEAR LAOCH DE CHUCHULAINN

Tar éis do Chúchulainn cú Chualainn a mharú, d'fhill sé ar Theach na mBuachaillí chun a chúrsa oiliúna a chríochnú. Lá amháin, bhí sé ins na coillte le scata buachaillí. Bhí siad ina suí ag caint le Chathbad, duine des na múinteoirí. Athair Rí Choncobhair abea Cathbad agus draoí abea é freisin — sé sin, saoi le comhachtaí draíochta. Le linn an chomhrá, d'iarr na buachaillí ar Chathbad a chomhachtaí draíochta a úsaid chun eolas d'fháil ar ce'n ghníomh a bheadh ámharach an lá sin. I dtosach báire, dhiúltaigh Cathbad, ach faoi dheireadh, dúirt sé leis na buachaillí go mbeadh an t-ádh le duine ar bith a thógfadh airm chogaidh do'n chéad uair an lá sin. Bheadh an duine sin láidir agus cáiliúil agus bheadh a ainm i mbéal na ndaoine go deo. Nuair a ceapadh go raibh an am tráthúil d'fhear óg bheith ina laoch tugadh airm dó don chéad uair. Uair speisialta dob ea an uair sin agus in aigne na ndaoine b'shin an lá a thóg sé airm suas.

Nuair a chuala Cúchulainn cad a bhí le rá ag Cathbad, bheartaigh sé a dhícheall a dhéanamh airm chogaidh a thógaint do'n chéad uair an lá sin. Chuaigh sé go dtí an rí agus dúirt sé: 'A Thiarna Rí; táim anseo chun a iarraidh ort airm chogaidh a thabhairt dom inniu. Tá gach rud a múintear i dTeach na mBuachaillí foghlamtha agam agus is mian liom anois bheith im laoch'.

D'fhéach Conchobhair air go géar agus chraith se a cheann. Gan aon amhras, buachaill beag tanaí abhí ina sheasamh os a chomhair amach, buachaill abhí i bhfad ó bheith ina fhear.

'Tá tú beag go leor fós,' a dúirt Conchobhair. 'Ba mhór an chabhair duit bheith beagáinín níos airde agus níos láidre'.

Bhí fearg ar Chúchulainn. 'Ní hé méid amháin atá tábhachtach imeasc laochra. Agus maidir le chomhacht, tabhair dom do shaighead fiaigh, a Thiarna, agus taispeáinfidh mé duit cad is comhacht ann'.

Thug Conchobhair dhá shaighead fiaigh dó. Thóg Cúchulainn iad agus bhris sé trasna a ghlúna iad fé mar ba bhrosna iad.

'Ní mhisde duit saighid níos fearr ná seo a thabhairt dom,' ar seiseann. Ansin, thug an rí dhá shaighead coghaidh dó.

Arís, bhris Cúchulainn iad gan stró agus chaith sé na smidiríní san aer.

Faoi'n am seo, bhí slua ag feachaint ar Chúchulainn. Sheas sé ina measc ag briseadh saighead agus claidheamh. Ansin, thug duine éigin carabad dó. Bhris sé an carabad seo agus morán charabad eile gan stró.

Faoi dheireadh thiar thall, bheartaigh Conchobhair deireadh a chur leis an spórt. Thóg sé amach na saighid agus na claidhimh ab fhearr dá raibh aige. Thug sé do Chúchulainn iad agus cé go ndearna Cúchulainn a dhícheall, theip air saighid agus claidhimh an rí a bhriseadh.

'Ós rud é gur theip ort iad a bhriseadh,' arsa an rí, 'is féidir leat iad a choiméad. Níl na hairm eile sáthach láidir duit. Anois, déan iarracht an carabad a bhriseadh'.

Léim Cúchulainn ar an gcarabad, ach theip air é a bhriseadh. Thóg sé na srianta, sheas sé sa charabad agus as go bráth leis na capaill. Bhi ionadh ar an rí nuair a chonaic sé go raibh smacht chómh maith ag Cúchulainn ar na capaill. Níor éirigh riamh roimhe sin le duine ar bith, ach amháin le fear chapaill an rí, smacht a choiméad ar na capaill chéanna. Tar éis tamaill de mharcaíocht, threoraigh Cúchulainn na capaill ar ais chuig an rí. Dúirt an rí:

'is féidir leat mo charabad agus na capaill a choiméad. Gan amhras, is an-laoch thú. Anois, ní mór duit cúl a thabhairt ar Theach na mBuachaillí'.

Agus sa slí sin, rinneadh laoch de Chúchulainn. Fé mar a dúirt Cathbad, laoch cáiliúil abea Cúchulainn de shíor ina dhiadh sin. Maireann a ainm i mbéal na ndaoine go dtí an lá atá inniu ann mar laoch láidir comhachtach.

88

Aerial view (above) of Tara, Co. Meath. Ancient seat of the high kings.

HORSE'S LEADING PIECE (below), found at Athymon, Co. Galway. It dates to 1st century B.C. Two ornamented portions of the same piece, cast in bronze, are shown. Diameters around 3 cm.

cuchulainn
in the land
of shadows

UCHULAINN HAD WON his place among the warriors. He was sixteen years old at this time and although he was small for his age, he was a handsome youth. One day he was at a feast in Tara, the home of the High King of Ireland. There he met a beautiful girl called Emer and he fell in love with her. In those days a man courted a girl only in her own house, so Cuchulainn decided that he would visit her as soon as possible and shortly after the feast he drove to her house in his chariot. Emer met him at the gate and welcomed him, but she would not let him enter the house because her father was not at home. Cuchulainn was able to speak to her though, he told her that he loved her and asked if she would marry him. Emer didn't refuse him outright but said that he would have to prove he was a great warrior first.

On his way home that day and on the next day and the day after Cuchulainn was very quiet. He was thinking of what Emer had said and wondering how he could do as she asked. At last he had an idea. He realised that he would have to learn more about the art of war. He had heard that there was a woman living in the Land of Shadows who was a very mighty warrior and a very good teacher. (Some say that the Land of Shadows was in Skye, an island off the coast of Scotland). Her name was Scatha. Cuchulainn decided to find this woman and ask her all that she knew about war and the skills of fighting.

Three days later, Cuchulainn set off on his journey to the Land of Shadows. It was a long journey over land and sea, but at last he arrived. Scatha's house was surrounded by a gulf filled with deep water which rushed in from the sea. There was a narrow bridge across this gulf joining Scatha's house to the surrounding countryside. In a hollow nearby Cuchulainn saw a cluster of little huts and a horse corral. Chariots, weapons and spear targets were scattered around the yard and some young men and boys were playing hurley nearby.

Cuchulainn walked towards them and as they saw him coming the game broke up. A tall fair-haired boy, who seemed to be leader of the group came to meet him. The boy had a hurley in his hand and he was followed by the rest of the group.

'You are welcome' he said. 'Have you come to join us?'

'Perhaps,' Cuchulainn replied. 'Where am I?'

The fair-haired boy answered him politely, pointing with his hurley. 'Scatha, the woman warrior, has a house over there. Her pupils live in the huts on this side of the river. We are some of her pupils – we have come to learn how to fight'.

'Then I will join you,' said Cuchulainn. 'I am Cuchulainn, a relative of King Conor of Ulster. I would also like to learn the arts of war from Scatha.'

'Good,' said the leader of the gang. 'We're glad to have another Irishman here. I am Ferdia, son of King Daman of Connaught. Come and have something to eat and drink and tell us all the latest news from Ireland'.

The boys left their game and crowded around Cuchulainn and they all went off to a big central hut where the slaves were preparing the evening meal.

After Cuchulainn had eaten and drunk with the boys, he went outside again with Ferdia. They looked across the gorge to Scatha's house and Cuchulainn asked:

'How can one get to Scatha's house?'

'No one can get over there' replied Ferdia. 'She comes over to us every morning, none of us have ever crossed the gorge'.

'Why is that?' asked Cuchulainn. 'If Scatha can cross the bridge to come over here, why can't we cross the bridge and go over to her?'

'That is a magic bridge,' replied Ferdia. 'It is called the Bridge of Leaps. Come and look at it'.

So they went together and looked at the bridge. It was formed out of a single piece of narrow rock and was smooth and slippery. They looked down into the gorge below where the waves were dashing against rocks on which great grey seals and sea-lions sprawled.

'It is nearly impossible to cross that bridge,' said Ferdia. 'If you step on the end of it, the middle springs up and flings you back. If you jump onto the centre of it you will almost certainly miss your footing and fall onto the rocks.'

But Cuchulainn wanted to see Scatha before morning, so he decided to try and cross the bridge. First, he would have a rest. So he and Ferdia went back to the huts where they slept for an hour or so. When they woke up it was night-time and there was a bright moon in the sky. They got up and set off towards the Bridge of Leaps. Most of the other boys followed them, laughing and jeering. They had heard that Cuchulainn was going to try to cross the Bridge of Leaps and they had come to have a good laugh at his failure.

When Cuchulainn came near the bridge, he threw off his cloak and began to run. At the very edge of the gulf he jumped, aiming for the centre of the bridge. But he didn't make it, and the bridge leapt upwards and flung him back among the boys who had come to watch and jeer. Furious, he jumped to his feet, ran for the bridge and jumped again. Again the bridge reared and threw him back. He tried again a third time and again he failed.

There was a roar of laughter from Ferdia and the boys. Ferdia called out to him as he struggled to his feet:

'Wait till the morning when Scatha comes over. She'll carry you back in her arms like a little dog'.

Ferdia's teasing infuriated Cuchulainn. Now he was determined to succeed. Running forward for the fourth time, he summoned up all his strength and jumped out over the gulf. The blood was pounding in his head and he could hardly

see the bridge. But this time he landed safely in the centre of the Bridge of Leaps and with another bound he was across.

He ran up to Scatha's house and knocked on the gate with his dagger. Watch-dogs barked at him and a voice called out to them to keep quiet. Then the gates were opened and in the light of torches which were carried by her attendants, Cuchulainn saw Scatha. She was a yellow-haired, thin-faced woman, wearing an old leather tunic and a short yellow kilt which barely reached her knees. She had bronze ornaments on her scarred arms. She stood leaning on a great spear with huge dogs crouching around her.

'Who are you?' she said to Cuchulainn, 'and why have you come to my house at this hour of the night?'

'I am Cuchulainn' he replied, 'and I have come to learn all that you can teach me about war and fighting'. 'Is that so,' said Scatha. 'When I saw you trying to jump the gorge I thought you must be the King of the Grasshoppers'. She laughed and sent him away saying: 'Go back to the other side now, you will find the bridge easier to cross this time. Don't try to jump across again until I show you how to do it properly — you wouldn't land safely a second time'.

Cuchulainn saluted her, turned on his heels and strode back to the Bridge of Leaps. This time, it was as broad and as easy to cross as a ditch.

When he reached the far side, Cuchulainn walked over to Ferdia, who was sitting on a rock.

'I made it,' he said, and reaching for the hunting knife in his belt, he added: 'Get up, Ferdia of Connaught. You cannot be afraid of the little dog that Scatha was to carry across the bridge. Now let's see which of the two of us is the stronger'.

Ferdia jumped to his feet and dived straight for Cuchulainn's knees. Cuchulainn, tired after his desperate leap, was off his guard. His feet went from under him and he fell down with a thud that winded him. Next instant, Ferdia was lying on top of him with his long legs twisted around Cuchulainn's, and his big hand pinning Cuchulainn's wrist to the grass. The other young warriors moved closer to see what would happen next. Gasping for breath, Cuchulainn clenched his teeth and struggled to get free. But he couldn't budge. Then suddenly he looked up and realised that Ferdia was laughing. 'Lie still,' said Ferdia — 'I am too young to die. And anyway, why should you attack me. If I hadn't teased you, you might never have crossed the bridge'.

Cuchulainn, seeing how strong Ferdia was, lay still. He thought of what Ferdia had said and realised that it was true. He had met his match in Ferdia. They got up and walked back to the hut together and ever afterwards Cuchulainn and Ferdia were firm friends. Before leaving the Land of Shadows they swore to be blood brothers, and to keep faith with each other as long as they lived.

PAGAN GOD. This carved stone head
was found at Pilltown, Co. Kilkenny, and
was probably the head of a pagan god. It
dates from around the 2nd or 1st century
B.C. Length of face: 20 cms.

the death of aife's only son

UCHULAINN HAD BEEN some time in the Land of Shadows, when war broke out between Scatha and Princess Aife, who was almost as great a warrior as Scatha herself. Cuchulainn fought in the war on Skatha's side and fought a duel with Aife. After a fierce struggle he took her captive but agreed not to kill her. Aife was kept by Scatha as a hostage, and during this time, Cuchulainn forgot Emer and loved and slept with Princess Aife. Before they parted, he gave her a ring and asked her if she had a son to send him to Ulster when his hand was big enough to fit the ring. He told her to call their son Connla and also asked her to put their son under a geis (promise) not to tell his name to anyone on his way to Ulster and never to refuse to fight a duel if he were challenged. Aife promised to do as Cuchulainn asked.

Twelve months later, Cuchulainn ended his training under Scatha and returned to Ulster where he fought many battles and won many victories. He did not visit Emer for many months after his return. Then one day, he heard that the King of Munster was courting her. Cuchulainn was determined that he and not the King would marry Emer, so he set out for her house with six chariots full of warriors, prepared to fight for her if he had to. Emer's father didn't approve of Cuchulainn and refused to let him enter the house — but this did not deter the young warrior. He attacked the house, killed the old man and carried his bride away by force — taking lots of gold and silver, fine weapons and jewellery as well.

Cuchulainn and Emer were married shortly afterwards. They lived happily together for many years but they had no children. Sometimes Cuchulainn felt sad about this and now and again he wondered whether the Princess Aife, whom he had loved many years before, had had a son.

One summer day, some years later, King Conor and some of his lords were racing their horses on the sea shore. They saw a small boat out on the sea, it was covered with plates of bronze, not skins, and was being rowed ashore by a handsome fair-haired boy. There was a small pile of stones in the boat and as the king and his lords watched, the boy put a stone into his sling and fired at one of the sea-birds flying overhead. He did not kill the bird, but brought it down alive into the boat. He did this again and again and knocked down many birds in this way. Then he lifted up the birds, patted them and threw them safely back into the sky. When he realised that he was being watched from the shore, he did a number of other unusual things, showing off to the king and his lords.

King Conor was watching the boy and became alarmed at his skill. As the boat came near the shore, the king turned to Cethern, son of Findtan, who was standing beside him, and said:

'Tell that boy not to land on this shore, but to go back to where he came from'.

Cethern went down to the water's edge and did as the king had asked him, but the boy refused to obey.

'This is a poor welcome for a stranger,' he said, 'but I will not go back'.

'The king says you must,' said Cethern.

But still the boy refused to obey. Cethern went back to the king and told him what had happened.

Then the king turned to Conall of the Victories and ordered him to go down to the water's edge.

'Go and see if you can make my message clearer,' he said.

'Use your sword if necessary'.

So Conall took out his sword and went down to the water's edge. The boy in the boat saw him coming. He fitted a stone into his sling and let fly at Conall with a loud shout. The stone knocked Conall down into the water. Before he could get up, the boy had reached him and had tied his hands behind his back.

Every warrior that the king sent down to the water's edge was treated in this way by the boy in the boat. At last the King decided to send for Cuchulainn who was at home with his wife. Cuchulainn jumped up immediately when the messenger arrived, but Emer caught his arm and asked him not to leave. When he asked her why he should stay at home she replied: 'I have a feeling that the boy on the seashore might be your son, sent to you by his mother, Aife. Do not go, for if you do, you might kill him'. But Cuchulainn kissed her and pulled her arms away, saying: 'Have sense, woman. The king has sent for me and I must go. Even if this young warrior is my son, Connla, I must kill him if necessary for the honour of Ulster'.

He immediately strapped on his sword, jumped onto his chariot and set off for the seashore, where the king and his lords were waiting. When he arrived on the shore, he saw the boy standing at the edge of the water. The boy was tossing up his spears and spinning them in the sunshine to amuse himself and pass the time. Cuchulainn jumped down from his chariot and walked towards the boy.

'Who are you and where do you come from?' asked Cuchulainn.

'That is something I may not tell you' answered the boy.

'You will regret those words' said Cuchulainn.

'That may be so,' said the boy, 'but I still may not tell'.

'Then you'd better get ready to die,' said Cuchulainn.

'I am ready' said the boy and immediately they both jumped into the shallow water. For a while, they fought with their swords and sparks flew from the blades and the sea-spray splashed about their legs. Cuchulainn knew that he had met his match in sword-fighting in this young boy. Suddenly, the boy flicked his wrist and neatly cut off a lock

of Cuchulainn's hair with his sword. With that, Cuchulainn threw away his sword and jumped on the boy. The boy threw away his sword too and jumped onto a flat slab of rock.

Cuchulainn pushed and pulled at the boy, but he could not move him one inch. They fought for a long time until at last they began to get tired. The boy began to lose his grip on the rock and suddenly with a cry and a splash they both fell into the water. The boy fell on top of Cuchulainn. His arms were around Cuchulainn and his knees were on Cuchulainn's chest holding him down under the water. Cuchulainn was near to drowning when he heard in the distance someone calling to him from the shore. It was his faithful charioteer, Laeg, who was about to throw a spear to his master. With a supreme effort, Cuchulainn tore one arm free and reaching out he caught the spear. It was his great spear, the Gae Bolga. Struggling desperately, Cuchulainn drew back his arm and stabbed the boy.

The waters around them gradually became red with the blood that flowed from the boy's wound. The boy loosed his grip and Cuchulainn was free. As the boy fell, mortally wounded, into the water, Cuchulainn put his arms around him and lifted him onto the rock. As he did so, he saw on the boy's finger the ring that he had given to Aife fifteen years before. And he knew that the boy who was now dying was his only son, Connla.

He took the boy in his arms and carried him out of the water and laid him on the sand in front of King Conor and his lords.

'Here is Connla, my son, for you,' he said, in a quiet voice. 'You have nothing to fear from him now'.

The boy stirred. 'Is that the king?' he asked.

'That is Conor, your kinsman and king of Ulster,' answered Cuchulainn, kneeling to support him.

'Tell me who the other warriors are?' demanded the boy. 'I have often talked with my mother about you and the Champions of the Red Branch and I would like to see them before I die'.

So one by one, the Red Branch Warriors came to kneel beside the boy and told him who they were. Then the boy said:

'I am glad that I have seen these great men'.

And he turned his face against his father's shoulder, cried out once and then he was dead.

The men of Ulster dug Connla's grave in the coarse grass near the shore and sorrowfully they buried him and set up his tomb-stone. And Cuchulainn was broken-hearted for he had slain his only son.

HOARD OF OBJECTS dating to 2nd century B.C. and found together just outside the bank of a Rath or Ring fort at Somerset, Co. Galway. Included are (top) a bronze ingot, (centre, from the left) portion of a bronze safety pin brooch, the handle of a small bronze cup, and a decorated bronze mount, (bottom) a bronze box with its lid containing, twisted up, a gold torc or neckring. Base of box (diameter) 12 cms.

103

Deirdre and the sons of usna

URING THE REIGN of King Conor Mac Nessa a child was born named Deirdre. Cathbad the Druid prophesied that she would bring sorrow to all Ulster. King Conor thought that he could prevent this by marrying Deirdre when she grew up, (Conor's first wife had died many years before) and in order to make sure that Deirdre wouldn't fall in love and marry somebody else, the king ordered that she be brought up in a very lonely place where she would never meet other people. He asked his old nurse, Levercham, to look after her.

Deirdre and the nurse went to live in a little house in a hidden valley in Slieve Gallion. The house had a roof of green sods and from the distance it looked like a little hill. Behind the house there was a garden with apple trees. Nobody ever came near the house except that once a year messengers from the king brought food and clothes to Deirdre and her nurse. Deirdre lived here until she was fifteen years old, and during these years she only saw her nurse, Levercham. When the king's messengers came with the food and clothes, Levercham would shut Deirdre in the house until the men had left. Every year the king sent a present to Deirdre. One year he sent a silver rattle hung with tiny bells of green glass. Another year he sent a dove in a cage. When Deirdre was older he sent her some beautiful silk that had come from a country half-way

104

around the world. When she was fourteen the king's present was a string of amber beads. He brought it himself and so for the first time, he saw Deirdre, and immediately fell in love with her. The king was quite an old man at this time and Deirdre was a very beautiful young girl.

Some months after the king's visit, a stranger came to the little house in the valley. It was a very wild night and the wind was roaring through the trees. Sleety rain lashed against the window as Deirdre was sitting at Levercham's feet spinning wool by the light of the turf fire. Suddenly, Deirdre heard a strange cry and lifted her head to listen.

'What was that,' she said to Levercham.

'Only a bird calling. It's nothing to worry about,' replied Levercham.

But the cry came again, nearer this time, and Deirdre said:

'It sounded like a human voice, the voice of someone in distress'.

Levercham replied: 'It is only the wild geese flying over. Stay by the fire and go on with your spinning'.

Then through the noise of the wind they both heard a knocking at the door. A voice cried out:

'Let me in, let me in'.

Deirdre jumped up and ran to open the door, ignoring the cries of Levercham who tried to stop her. The door swung open and the wind and rain swept into the house. And out of the wind and rain, a man stumbled in, drenched from top to toe. He helped Deirdre to close the door against the storm and then he came in to the fire. Levercham took one look at him and said:

'It is Naisi, the son of Usna'. Then turning to him, she said:

'Why are you here? This is not the time of year for bringing food and clothing. You know you shouldn't come here'.

'I know that,' said Naisi, 'I know that no one but the king is allowed to come here, but I had to get shelter some-where from the storm. I was hunting with my brothers, Ardan and Ainle, and they went home before I was ready.

I stayed out too long and I was trapped by the storm. Please let me sit by your fire until the storm dies down. I am very cold and wet and weary'.

'Very well,' said Levercham, 'sit down by the fire and have something to eat and drink. If I turned you away now you would be dead by morning'.

So Naisi sat down by the fire, and Deirdre brought food and drink and set it down beside him. When Naisi looked up at Deirdre and saw how beautiful she was, he fell in love with her at once. Deirdre, unaccustomed as she was to strangers, couldn't look away from this handsome young man. Levercham saw what was going on and said to herself:

'I can see trouble ahead. Naisi is a handsome young man and Deirdre's eyes are bright with love for him. I should have turned him away to die in the storm'.

But Levercham did not interfere. Although she had great respect for King Conor, she felt sad at the thought of Deirdre marrying a man old enough to be her father.

The next morning the storm had blown over and Naisi went away. But during the following months he often visited the little house in the valley. He had fallen in love with Deirdre and had to see her, although he knew that the king would be very angry if he knew of these visits. Levercham also knew, but she didn't tell the king what was going on.

One evening in early spring when Naisi came to visit her, Deirdre turned to him and said:

'Take me with you. I don't want to marry the king. I want to marry you'.

Naisi groaned. 'How can I do that, I am one of the king's own bodyguards. He would never forgive me if I went away with you'.

That evening, as he returned home, Naisi vowed in his heart that he would not visit Deirdre again, but he soon found that he could not live without seeing Deirdre. Again and again he visited her. He could not stay away.

Some months later, the king announced that he would marry Deirdre in a few weeks. Naisi had to decide whether he would take Deirdre away or not. At last he decided that he would leave the king's service. He would marry Deirdre and flee across the sea with her to another country although this would bring him disgrace and dishonour among his own people. He said to Deirdre:

'Let us go. There are other lands across the sea and other kings to serve. It will be worth it, if you love me, Deirdre'.

When it was dark the following night he came with horses and with his two brothers, Ardan and Ainle. They collected Deirdre and Levercham because the old nurse said:

'I have been disloyal to the king. I dare not stay here now'.

After a lot of travelling they settled across the sea in a place called Glen Etive on the shores of a lake. Here they lived for a number of years. The men hunted and Deirdre and Levercham cooked and spun and wove wool from the sheep. And back in Ireland, the king of Ulster was angry and he did not forgive nor forget what the sons of Usna had done, but sent spies after them to find out what they were doing.

One day, about four years after Naisi and Deirdre had left Ireland, King Conor sent for Conall of the Victories, Cuchulainn and Fergus MacRoy and said to them:

'I think it is time to bring home the sons of Usna'.

'Will you forgive them?' asked Cuchulainn.

'Yes, I will,' said the king. 'I was angry at first when they took Deirdre away. But I have decided to forgive them'.

So he sent Fergus MacRoy across the sea to Glen Etive to tell Naisi and his brothers that they were forgiven and to ask them to come back to Ulster.

When Fergus MacRoy arrived at Glen Etive, Naisi and his brothers were overjoyed to hear that the king had forgiven them. But Deirdre was afraid and didn't really believe in Conor's change of heart. She wanted to stay in Scotland. She said:

'I find it hard to believe that the king has forgiven us. What guarantee have we that he will not harm us if we return?'

Fergus MacRoy replied: 'You have my word for it'.

That evening Deirdre and Naisi and his brothers invited Fergus to eat with them and next morning they gathered up all their belongings and set off for Ireland. When they arrived in Ulster, Baruch, one of King Conor's warriors, met them.

Baruch invited Fergus to eat with him and Fergus was obliged to accept this invitation. Fergus MacRoy's sons, Illan the Fair and Buinne the Red agreed to accompany the sons of Usna and Deirdre and Levercham on the rest of the journey to King Conor's home in Emain Macha. When they arrived in Emain Macha, they were asked to stay at the Red Branch Hostel until the king sent for them.

After some time the king sent for Levercham. She made her peace with the king and then he asked her about Deirdre

'Is she still as beautiful as ever?' he asked.

'Indeed no,' she answered. 'Life in the wilderness is hard on a woman. Her complexion is no longer lily-white. The wind has chapped her lips and her hair is faded from the sun. She is no longer the beautiful Deirdre that you knew in the valley in Slieve Gallion'.

When Levercham had left him, the king began to wonder whether she had told him the truth. So he sent one of his warriors to the Red Branch Hostel to look secretly and see whether Deirdre was as weather-beaten as Levercham had said she was.

That evening, Deirdre and Naisi were playing chess together in the Red Branch Hostel. Suddenly Naisi saw a face peeping in at the window. It was the king's messenger who was spying on Deirdre. Naisi picked up one of the chessmen from the board and threw it at the messenger. It struck the messenger on the face and knocked out his left eye. The man fell to the ground and ran back to the king with blood pouring down his face.

'The woman in the Red Branch Hostel is the most beautiful woman I have ever seen,' he said.

King Conor was furious. He stormed into the great hall where his warriors were eating and shouted at them to bring the three sons of Usna to him, alive or dead.

'They are traitors,' he shouted. 'They have wronged me and I will have my revenge'.

The warriors jumped up and snatching their weapons they ran out shouting. When passing the fires, some of them pulled out flaming branches and whirled them above their heads as they ran. Naisi and the others in the hostel saw the red flicker of the flames through the windows and heard the shouting. Immediately Naisi jumped up and locked the door. Then snatching their weapons, Naisi and his brothers ran to the windows. For a while there was silence in the hall. Then Celthair, son of Uthica called to them to come out.

Naisi and his brothers refused to obey, but they couldn't stay in the Hostel for very long. Soon someone shouted:

'Burn them out; burn them out'.

The shouting got louder and the warriors shoved their blazing branches under the thatch. Deirdre cried out when she saw the red flames running among the rafters and the hall began to fill with smoke.

Then Naisi said:

'It is time to open the door for it is better to die by the sword than by fire'.

So they opened the door and went out to meet the king's warriors. There was a great fight and many of the warriors of Ulster were killed by the sons of Usna, and the sons of Fergus MacRoy. But in the fighting, Illan the Fair was killed and then the king's followers bribed Buinne the Red to leave his friends.

But at last the sons of Usna had to surrender. The king's warriors surrounded them and took the swords from their hands. They captured them and tied them up and dragged them before King Conor. Then the king called for one of his warriors to come forward and slay the three, but no one was willing to do this. At last, Owen, prince of Ferney stepped forward and took up Naisi's own sword from the ground where it lay.

'Kill the three of us at one blow,' said Naisi then. 'The sword is strong enough for that, and so we shall all die at the same time'.

As they stood there side by side, with their arms tied behind them, the prince of Ferney cut off their three proud heads at one stroke. Then Deirdre broke free of the men who held her and casting herself upon the three headless bodies she cried out:

'O sons of Usna, the days will be long and lonely now that you are dead. I cannot live without you. O young men

111

digging the grave, leave space there for me to follow, for I am sad and sorry and do not wish to live any longer'.

And as they tried to drag her away from Naisi's body, she grabbed a little sharp knife from the belt of one of her captors. With a last sorrowful cry, she thrust the blade into her breast. Deirdre was dead.

Deirdre and Naisi were buried close together and near their grave the great church of Armagh was later built. Out of Deirdre's grave and out of Naisi's there grew two tall yew trees. When these trees were fully grown they met above the church roof. When the wind hushed through the branches, the people said:

'Deirdre and Naisi are singing together'.

NINE PINS (above), all cast from bronze and dating from the 2nd century B.C. They were mainly used to hold the dress in place but occasionally were used in the hair. Pin on right 12 cms. long.

SPUN BRONZE CUP (below) with a raised zig-zag pattern on the rim. The handle is cast in the form of a stylised bird's head and neck. From Keshcarrigan, Co. Leitrim, it dates to 1st century B.C. About 14.5 cms.

maeve
of cruachan

AEVE AND AILELL were Queen and King of Connaught. (In that province the chieftain-ship of the land passed from mother to daughter and the King wasn't so important). One night as they were lying in bed they began to talk about their possessions. Ailell began by telling Maeve how much better off she was now married to him since he was a wealthy man – Maeve was furious at this and told him she had been a rich woman before she met him. Her father had left her the whole province of Cruachan and she had more possessions than he. Ailell wouldn't believe this, so they decided to count up everything that they owned. They took out all their house-hold goods, jugs, basins, bowls and drinking cups, they counted all their jewellery and clothes, they counted all their animals – sheep, pigs and cattle. Each time they found that their possessions were equal. If Maeve had a fine silk cloak, so did Ailell. If she had a magnificent horse – so did he. Only in one thing did they differ. Ailell had a magnificent strong, white bull in his herd. This bull was called Finnbennach – he had been a calf to one of Maeve's cows but had left to join Ailell's herd because he didn't want to follow a woman. Maeve had no bull as good as this white one and she was heartbroken to see Ailell beating her. She was so upset that she asked one of her men, MacRoth to see

if he knew if there was a bull to match the white one anywhere in the country. MacRoth told her that Daire MacDiachna in Ulster owned a great brown bull called Donn Cuailnge who could match Ailell's white one, so Maeve immediately sent MacRoth to ask Daire to lend her the brown bull for a year. She promised that the bull would be returned to him at the end of that time with fifty young heifers as well in payment for the loan.

Daire was delighted when he heard this offer and agreed to lend his brown bull to Maeve. Then he promised food, wine and a comfortable resting place for the messengers from Connaught. As they were relaxing and enjoying this hospitality the men began to talk — one of them said 'Surely there is no man in Ulster better than Daire?' The other replied 'Conor the King is a better man, still it was good of Daire to give us the brown bull. It would have needed all the men of Ireland to take it away by force'.

At that moment one of Daire's men came into the room and heard what they were saying. He turned around straight away and went to look for his leader to see if the story was true. He asked Daire whether the brown bull had been given to Maeve, and found that it had.

'That was very foolish behaviour not worthy of a king. The messengers were right in what they said. If you hadn't given the bull up freely he would have been taken by force.' Daire was furious and said 'Nothing leaves here unless I choose to let it go'.

The messengers got up early the next day and went to collect the bull so that they could drive it back to Connaught — but Daire refused to tell them where it was, saying 'You must go back to Connaught empty-handed. Think yourselves lucky that you are still alive — I only spared you because you were visitors'.

When they asked him why he had changed his mind, he answered 'You said that if I didn't give the bull up freely Ailell and Maeve would have brought their war host into Ulster. I'm not going to hand over my bull this time unless I have to'.

The messengers tried to talk him round saying that they

had drunk too much and shouldn't be held responsible for statements they had made, but Daire remained firm. The messengers had to go back empty-handed.

When Maeve heard this story she said:

'Well, Daire must have known what would happen if he refused our request. We will march against Ulster and capture the bull'.

HORSE BIT, cast in bronze, and ornamented with slightly raised curved patterns – it is typically Irish in style and dates to 3rd century B.C. Length: 26.5 cm.

the hosting of maeve

AEVE STARTED TO make plans for a cattle raid on Ulster. She ordered all the tribes of Connaught to get ready for war. From all over Connaught, the warriors and chieftains began to gather. They were headed by the seven sons of Maeve, each with their own armies. Kat and Anluan, the sons of Maga, came with three thousand men. A host of the men of Leinster followed their king who was Ailell's brother. Ferdia came with his army, from Connaught, though his heart was heavy, remembering how he and Cuchulainn had sworn to be friends when they were leaving Scatha's training school. Cormac, son of King Conor, and Fergus MacRoy, and those others who had left Emain Macha after the deaths of Deirdre and the sons of Usna, were already in Roscommon.

Ulster seemed doomed to lose the war. Many years before, the province had been cursed by a dying woman – half-human and half-fairy. At her death, she had cursed the men of Ulster with the words:

'O warriors of Ulster, at the time when you most need your strength, when the enemy is near, may the weakness of a dying woman come upon you'.

And so it had been ever since. And now, Conor the king himself, lay ill at Emain Macha. His son Cuscrid, and Owen prince of Ferney and even Conall of the Victories lay

119

moaning on their beds with not even enough strength in them to lift a spear. All the Red Branch Warriors except Cuchulainn were stricken by this weakness.

Cuchulainn was not affected by the curse because his father Lugh, who was a Sun God, was not a man of Ulster. Cuchulainn was at Ard Cuillen on the southern borders of Murthemeny, settling some dispute between two of his chieftains, when the Great Weakness struck. He heard the thunderous noise of weapons and chariots being prepared and he knew that war had been declared on Ulster and that until the other men regained their strength he was the only one who could defend the province.

Cuchulainn and his charioteer Laeg, the only other man to escape the sickness, protected all the passes into Ulster against Maeve and her armies. This situation continued for some time but Maeve finally demanded a meeting.

Maeve and Cuchulainn stood and faced each other across a narrow glen in the foothills of Slieve Cuillen. Maeve was surrounded by chiefs and captains. She carried her spear in her hand and she wore a golden crown on her head.

There was no one with Cuchulainn except Laeg, his charioteer. Maeve was amazed when she saw him. She found it hard to believe that this small dark man, who was like a war-god rather than a warrior, should be the terror of her whole army. Maeve and Cuchulainn then started to discuss whether they could agree to end the war without further fighting. They spent all day discussing this matter. At last, leaning on his spear, Cuchulainn called across the glen:

'We have been discussing this matter all day and I'm tired. This is my final offer. Listen carefully. There is a ford across the river about an hour's drive north of here. I'll guard this ford and you can send your champions to fight me one at a time. Each day, while the fight lasts, your army may go forward into Ulster, but at the end of each combat the army must stop wherever it is and wait until the next day. These are my terms Maeve, don't refuse them lightly'.

Maeve thought for a long while, leaning also on her spear. Then she lifted her head and shouted back across the glen:

'All right, Cuchulainn, I agree'.

120

So Cuchulainn stood at the ford and that evening Maeve sent out the first of her champions. They fought in the shallow waters of the ford. But Maeve's army had hardly moved an inch from their last night's camp before their champion went down with Cuchulainn's spear through his heart. The army had to camp on the same spot that night. The next day, Maeve sent her second champion into battle. Before Maeve's army had moved three spear throws farther north, the second champion had been killed. Champion after champion came, and Cuchulainn met and killed each one. Each time, Maeve's army advanced while the fight lasted, and halted and made camp for the night when the fighting ended.

Finally, Maeve decided to send out Fergus MacRoy to the ford – but he was Cuchulainn's foster father and they had no desire to fight each other.

When Cuchulainn saw who it was, a cold sweat came over him. But there was a twinkle in Fergus's eyes, and when they came together in the middle of the ford, Fergus whispered to Cuchulainn:

'Will you run away today, Cuchulainn, if I run away another day?'

Cuchulainn replied:

'Yes, I will. That is a fair bargain. But remember, I'll choose the time when you must run away from me'.

Then they attacked each other with such ferocity that those looking on thought that they fought to the death. After a while, Cuchulainn allowed Fergus to knock the broad spear from his hand and he sprang back with a cry and he turned and ran.

And all of Maeve's army shouted and drummed their spears on their shields with excitement. The fight was over for that day and Fergus swaggered back to stand beside the queen's chariot. They made camp for another night, and in the morning sent yet another champion to the ford.

But Maeve, furious that one man should hinder her progress, had made a plan. She broke her promise to Cuchulainn and while he was fighting at the ford, Maeve left her army behind and drove into Ulster with a few of her best warriors. There was no one to stop her because Cuchulainn had his hands full at the ford and the other Ulstermen were still weak with sickness. She went north, towards Armagh, plundering and burning the houses and lands that she passed. At last she reached the glens of Slieve Cuillen where the brown bull was grazing with his herd, so she captured him and drove him off.

Now Cuchulainn had finished that day's fight, and he was hunting for food in the countryside (Cuchulainn and Laeg had to hunt for themselves; though Maeve's army had the whole country to supply them). Suddenly Cuchulainn saw Maeve driving the brown bull away. He rushed to the rescue, but though he killed many men, he wasn't able to free the bull and it was driven south into Connaught.

Cuchulainn did not dare follow because he had to defend the ford. He knew that Maeve would still keep up the attack on Ulster. And indeed she did, in fact she forgot altogether the promise that she had made and sent her champions to fight Cuchulainn in bands of ten and twenty at a time instead of singly. As a result Cuchulainn was wounded many times and he became tired and weak.

One morning, knowing he could not hold out much longer, Cuchulainn sent his charioteer, Laeg, to Emain Macha to see if he could rouse the warriors of Ulster from their weakness. By evening, Laeg had not returned and Cuchulainn made his own fire and lay down with his cloak about him as usual. He felt sad and weary and missed hearing Laeg whistle as he tidied up the camp. For a while he lay watching the camp fires of the enemy across the river. Then he looked at his own small fire, and he began to lose heart. And as he watched he saw a man walking through the great Connaught camp. No one stirred nor turned to look as he went by. He wore a gold tunic and a green cloak held in place by a big silver brooch. He carried a black and silver shield in one hand and in the other were two spears. He came straight down to the ford and crossed over to Cuchulainn's camp. Cuchulainn remembered suddenly where he had seen the man before.

The stranger came and bent over him and said:

'You have fought a hard fight, and there is more fighting yet to do. Sleep now, Cuchulainn, sleep, for three days and

three nights'.

'And who will hold the ford?' asked Cuchulainn.

'I will hold the ford, but everyone will still think it is you,' replied the man.

And Cuchulainn knew that Lugh his father had come to help him in his greatest need. Then he fell into a deep, deep sleep. And as he slept, Lugh, the Sun Lord, healed his wounds, and defended the ford.

Meanwhile, in Emain Macha, Cuchulainn's charioteer, Laeg had failed to rouse the king and his men. But in the Boys' House, life continued as usual, for the Great Weakness fell only upon grown men. When the boys in training heard from Laeg how difficult it was for Cuchulainn their hero, they took up their weapons and set off to help him. Some took the chariots and horses from the stables, and they marched off to meet Maeve's army.

At last they reached the enemy camp. Three times they attacked and at each charge, they killed a large number of the enemy host. But at each charge there were fewer left of the Boys' Band until there were only a handful left. They continued to press forward at their young captain's heels, bravely attacking the enemy, until at last there were none of the boys left alive.

All this happened while Cuchulainn lay in his tranced sleep. When he woke, feeling well and strong as though he had never been at battle, he saw the Boys' bodies scattered on the ground and he realised what had happened.

He was overcome with anger and sorrow and he vowed to take his revenge. He armed himself and harnessed his horses who were grazing nearby. But this time he wouldn't wait for the enemy to come to him. This time he, Cuchulainn would attack the enemy. He did not charge straight upon the enemy troops, but shouting and roaring at his horses, he galloped around and around the army. His chariot wheels were red hot, and ploughed the earth like a mighty plough. With dashing strokes of his great spear, he killed all before him. The curved war-blades on the chariot-wheels caught and mangled the enemy until bodies were piled high on each other. And as Cuchulainn attacked the enemy, the wind rose and darkness covered the land. And only when night began to fall and when his horses were worn out and weary, did Cuchulainn stop fighting. Almost two hundred chiefs and princes of the enemy as well as many lesser warriors died that day.

This was called for ever after the 'Slaughter of Murthemeny', — the slaughter that Cuchulainn made in revenge for the death of the Boys' Band.

BRONZE MOUNT This beautiful ornamental mount dates from about the 5th or 6th century A.D. and was cast in bronze. It was then worked deeper by hand and decorated with red enamel. Diameter: 5 cms.

127

the death
of ferdia

NE EVENING IN THE camp Queen Maeve sent a message to Ferdia asking him to come and see her. He went very unwillingly because he guessed what she might be about to ask him. Maeve was sitting on cushions beside a fire leaning up against her chariot and for a time she just looked at Ferdia as if she didn't know what to say. Then she said 'Ferdia, I know that you are a friend of Cuchulainn's so I haven't asked you to go down to fight him like the other champion warriors – but you are the only one of our great warriors left so you will have to pick up your weapons and go down to fight'.

Ferdia replied: 'If you know that Cuchulainn and I are friends, then you must know that I am not going to do as you ask – even though you are Queen of Connaught Cuchulainn is like a brother to me.' Maeve tried to persuade him and even offered him her daughter in marriage. (This meant that eventually Ferdia would be King of Connaught after Ailell's death). But still Ferdia refused to go. Then Maeve became angry and said to Ferdia 'Do you realise that you are the only one of my warriors who has refused to go out and fight. You say that you don't want to go because Cuchulainn is a friend, but probably the real reason is that you are afraid'.

Ferdia said that the other warriors all knew that he wasn't

a coward, but Maeve continued to jibe at him, reminding him of all the fighting men who had already died in battle and told him that nobody would ever associate with him again; if he deserted his people when they needed help he would be completely dishonoured.

Ferdia grew white as he listened to her, and then suddenly became angry and stormed out of the tent. He found his charioteer and told him to have the chariot ready early next morning because he was going down to fight at the ford. This news spread through the camp like wildfire and Ferdia's men were saddened because they didn't think that he would come back alive.

Ferdia went down to the ford at dawn on the following morning and as there wasn't any sign of Cuchulainn he settled down to sleep until he should arrive. Some hours later he was wakened by the sound of a war chariot — Cuchulainn raced up, stopped on the far side of the ford and looked across at Ferdia. He said 'So it is you, Ferdia — I never thought you would come to fight me'.

Ferdia shouted back 'Why shouldn't I come? — I belong to Connacht as well'.

'Yes, but don't you remember the time when we were training to be warriors with Skatha — we were always together, hunting and feasting, sharing the same cup and the same bed'

Ferdia was upset, but said 'Don't talk of our friendship, we must forget that now, we are here to fight'.

Cuchulainn agreed reluctantly and asked Ferdia to choose the weapons for the fight. He decided to use javelins and for the rest of the morning they hurled these at each other, but they were both able to defend themselves with shields and neither was wounded. In the afternoon they used heavy spears but again neither of them hurt the other seriously.

When evening came they stopped fighting — threw their weapons to their charioteers and ran towards each other and embraced. That night they shared their food, dressed each other's wounds and settled down, with their charioteers to sleep in the same place.

On the second day Cuchulainn chose the weapons and

they spent the day fighting from their chariots with great stabbing spears. When night came they were both exhausted and cut and bleeding but still evenly matched. But that night was spent together in friendship like the one before, sharing their food and putting healing ointments on each other's wounds. Cuchulainn said to Ferdia that surely it wasn't worth ending such a friendship just to win Ailell and Maeve's daughter in marriage. Ferdia was saddened at this and said 'I am not fighting you so that I can marry Findabair — but because I would have been shamed and dishonoured throughout Connaught if I had refused'.

On the next morning it was Ferdia's turn again to choose the weapons and they fought all day with their heavy iron swords and wounded each other severely. That night they didn't talk and stayed on opposite sides of the ford. When Ferdia woke up next morning he realised that this would be his last day fighting and he armed himself carefully. He was afraid that Cuchulainn would use the gae bolga so he tied a great flat stone across his belly and covered it with an iron plate, he put on his war helmet and a silken tunic and went to meet Cuchulainn, and as he waited he practised tossing his javelin.

Cuchulainn watched him sadly, because he also knew that this would be the last day's fighting. He asked Laeg, his charioteer to watch the fight and to spur him on with insults if he seemed to be weakening.

It was Cuchulainn's turn to name the weapons and he said that anything could be used. They fought with spears and then with swords in the ford. Three times Cuchulainn leapt at Ferdia to attack him, but each time Ferdia knocked him off with his shield. Laeg began to mock Cuchulainn saying 'Don't call yourself a warrior — see how easily he can throw you off — women would laugh to see you'.

When he heard this, Cuchulainn's battle frenzy seized him and he gained strength and began to fight like a demon.

For a time the two warriors grappled desperately with each other. Then, suddenly Cuchulainn lost his footing and Ferdia stabbed him in the shoulder and slashed at him repeatedly with his sword. Cuchulainn shouted to Laeg to throw him the gae bolga and though Ferdia tried to protect himself with his shield the terrible spear struck him. It shattered the stone and entered deep into his body and he collapsed dying. Cuchulainn caught him as he fell and carried him to the bank; then he fainted beside the body of his friend. Laeg tried to get him to move to safety before Maeve's army came sweeping down to avenge Ferdia, but Cuchulainn was heartbroken and weeping, he had killed his dearest friend. In the end, Laeg had to use force to push him into the chariot and take him away from the ford.

THE END OF THE CATTLE RAID

Cuchulainn lay sick for many days after his fight with Ferdia, weak and depressed and not aware of what was happening — but in the meantime the men of Ulster had recovered from their great weakness and had assembled their war host to go and fight against Queen Maeve. Fergus MacRoy fought beside Maeve at the head of the Connaught men and found himself facing his old comrades from Ulster. (He had left Ulster because of a quarrel with King Conor over the deaths of Deirdre and the sons of Usna). The two armies joined in fierce battle. The noise of the battle travelled for many miles and reached the place where Cuchulainn was lying sick. Suddenly, as he heard the sounds of fighting he seemed to become strong and rose up out of his bed, calling for his weapons and his chariot. He then rode into the battle shouting his war cry which struck terror and fear into the hearts of those who heard it. In the middle of the field he found Fergus MacRoy and Cuchulainn yelled out to him above the noise. 'Remember to keep your half of the bargain we made at the ford'. Fergus stood still, then he said, 'Yes, I'll keep the bargain,' and turned and left the field. When the warriors saw Fergus, one of their leaders leaving the battle they became uneasy and the men from Munster and Leinster left also, so Maeve was only left with her warriors from Connaught. They fought bravely but were no match for Cuchulainn once his battle fury was on him, and by the end of the day they were in retreat, with the men from Ulster in pursuit. Cuchulainn was following the retreating warriors closely when he suddenly found Queen Maeve crouched beside her chariot which had broken — he could have killed her easily but she begged for mercy and Cuchulainn let her live saying that he didn't kill women. He put her into a new chariot and sent her back to Connaught, he knew it would be many years before they would dare to raid cattle again.

Though Maeve had driven the brown bull down into Connaught it was never of any benefit to her. Ailell's white bull was determined to keep his lordship of the herd, and attacked the brown bull immediately. The fight between the two bulls was a terrible one, the air was filled with their bellows and the ground itself shook under their hooves. Finally the brown bull trampled on the white bull and killed him; as he rushed around bellowing in triumph, the brown bull himself fell to the ground, dead.

Maeve was not really willing to admit defeat but Ailell her husband, knowing the sadness and loss that had been caused by the raid insisted that a seven year peace be made with Ulster in both their names. This was done and the Cattle Raid ended.

THE DEATH OF CUCHULAINN

The peace between Ulster and Connaught was kept for seven years, but Maeve never forgave Cuchulainn for the shame and loss that he had brought upon her. Some years later she called all those in Ireland who hated Cuchulainn to march with their war hosts against Ulster. The great weakness had struck again and Cuchulainn was left alone to guard the border pass. He fought terribly but was heavily outnumbered and was badly wounded. Cuchulainn finally realised that he was dying and asked his enemies if they would let him go down to the lakeside to drink. They agreed provided that he would return — Cuchulainn said that if he didn't come back they could come down and fetch what was left of him.

Cuchulainn wrapped himself in his cloak and staggered down to the waterside. He washed his wounds, drank and then prepared to die. He was too weak to climb back but he knew they would come looking for him eventually. He was too weak to stand unaided but wanted to die honourably on his feet, so he managed to tie himself to a large stone that was standing beside the lake. His enemies came down but they just stood looking, not one of them dared to attack him again.

Cuchulainn's horse, the Grey of Macha, came back to be with his master, and began attacking and killing the on-lookers with his hooves and teeth.

Finally a great black crow flew down and settled on Cuchulainn's shoulder and they knew then that he was dead. One of the warriors came up and cut off Cuchulainn's head — he was going to give it to Maeve but though she normally didn't mind bloodshed, on this occasion she turned away in horror and wouldn't touch it. Though she had survived Cuchulainn it was a poor victory.

ROTARY QUERN for grinding corn. The picture shows the upper stone only, and it is from Kilmacaran, Co. Cavan. Dates to early Christian period, 7th or 8th century A.D. Breadth: 44.5 cms.

135

ACKNOWLEDGEMENTS

We would like to thank Áine Hyland, Anne Gill and Brian Kavanagh for work in the development of the materials: Tim O'Neill for reading and commenting on the manuscript, the Editor of the Proceedings of the Royal Irish academy for permission to quote from J. J. Tierney, "The Celtic Ethnology of Posidonius" (P.R.I.A., 1960), Mrs. Sheehy for kind permission to include The Hermit's Song, The King of Connaught, Jealousy, and Oisín, from Kings Lords & Commons by Frank O'Connor published by Macmillan of London; Dr. Brendan Kennelly for kind permission to include The Old Woman of Beare, A Love Song and My Story. We would like to thank Dr. Joseph Raftery, Director of the National Museum of Ireland for his generous assistance.

ILLUSTRATIONS

We are grateful to the following for permission to reproduce the illustrations in Celtic Society (The Celtic Way of Life and The Ulster Cycle). All the photographs are courtesy of the National Museum of Ireland except on page 61, courtesy Commissioners of Public Works, Ireland and page 17 courtesy Dr. J. K. St. Joseph, University of Cambridge. The photographs on pages 19 and 21 are by kind permission of the Craggaunowen Project, Shannon Free Airport Development Company Ltd. We thank Alf Mac Lochlainn, Director of the National Library of Ireland for permission to reproduce the map on page 8.

In a few instances we have not succeeded in making contact with copyright holders and would be grateful if they would write to the publishers.